Kidversation

Connect with your kids, one conversation at a time

Scott Stamper, MPA

Founder of Families in Recovery, Inc.

Kidversation
Helping you connect with your kids, one conversation at a time

Check us out on the web at kidversation.com

Kidversation
Text copyright © 2011 by Scott Stamper

Published by KoobEbook Publishing
Learn more: koobebook.com

- ISBN-13:978-0615518824 (Koobebook)
- ISBN-10:0615518826

If I had my child to raise all over again,
I'd build self-esteem first, and the house later.
I'd finger-paint more, and point the finger less.
I would do less correcting and more connecting.
I'd take my eyes off my watch, and watch with my eyes.
I'd take more hikes and fly more kites.
I'd stop playing serious, and seriously play.
I would run through more fields and gaze at more stars.
I'd do more hugging and less tugging.

~ Diane Loomans, from "If I Had My Child To Raise Over Again"

What a child doesn't receive he can seldom later give.

~ P.D. James

CONTENTS

Enjoyment

Family

School

INTRODUCTION

Oh, to be a parent. It is one of life's greatest thrills. I am reminded on a daily basis why parenting is the best job on the world. Maybe it is Quinn asleep in my lap while I am working on my laptop. Maybe it is Ella pulling my wife and me into a dance party in the living room. Or perhaps it is Rowan running into the kitchen and in his best little voice, belting out "Jingle Bells" in February.

And oh to be a parent. It is also one of life's greatest challenges. Reminders for this also come frequently – Quinn smacking his brother on the head or Ella tantruming over homework or Rowan crying over who knows what this time.

When done right, parenting challenges us to be the best selves we can be. It gives us the opportunity to rise above the daily challenges we all face in order to really be present. Raising kids takes our ego, our sense of self, and says "You might have existed as a strong-willed, independent person before, but now you are a puppet!" Mary and I often joke that we have not had a real night's sleep in 7 years. And many mornings we often think back to savoring cups of coffee and the newspaper, usually while a stray foot kicks my coffee over onto the newspaper I've not even had time to open.

The simple fact is, we all enter the delivery room (or "adoption room" as the case may be) one person, and when we come out, we've been reborn into this new creature called a parent.

Husband goes in. Wife goes in. Mom, dad, and baby come out. Buy one birth, get two rebirths free.

And what are we reborn into? Raise your hand if you've ever wiped your kid's nose on your sleeve (or hat, or sock, or whatever article of clothing is nearest). Raise your hand if you've ever yelled at your teen for answering a question you asked them (to paraphrase Bill Cosby, "Don't you answer me when I'm asking you a question.") Raise your hand if you've ever had your kids dressed, 100% ready to go out, and still found yourself trying to get out the door ½ hour later due to bathroom emergencies, lost clothes/toys/MP3 players.

That's right – we are reborn into varying degrees of insanity.

I would never want to give the impression I think parenting is anything less than miraculous. It is the greatest gift our kids can ever give us, to teach them, help them, parent them. But I also don't think it is helpful to approach parenting with anything less than a sober view of how things can really be.

For many of us, there are times when it feels like kids exists for no other reason than to play bongos on our psyche. This is not actually the truth - we matter far less to them then their own gigantic egos and their search for self-definition and growth. The simple fact is, for most kids, the very act growing up is really tough. They face daily challenges that would make most grown-ups weep.

Children, from grade school through college face so many challenges, as parents we should marvel at their strength. Imagine showing up at work and finding out that your co-worker is no longer talking to you because she is now best friends with another co-worker and now they are telling lies to get everyone else at work to hate you as well. Or imagine showing up and having your boss sit you down and tell you that you are practically failing at all of your work and that your future will be terrible as a result, and then getting that message reinforced daily.

The truth is that kids have it pretty tough on so many fronts. It's easy for adults to look back on childhood and only focus on the parts that seemed great. Maybe it was all the free time, or perhaps the sports, or just not seeming like there was as much pressure as there is now. But the reality is that kids of all ages are dealing with more pressures, daily struggles, and challenges than their growing and developing minds can cope with effectively – at least without your help. That is where we come in!

It might be a bit goofy, but we parents should see ourselves as superheroes. Even if our kids think we are the villains. Our job is to help them learn, grow, and think for themselves in a meaningful way. At the same time, we must prevent them from making the worst of the bad choices, and then find ways to help them help themselves when they do. Oh yeah, and we have to do it while maintaining some semblance of our own sanity and while actually having lives of our own. Like I said, superheroes.

Maybe a metaphor will help. Think for a moment about air travel. What does it take to have a successful flight? You arrive at the airport, go through the security check in, find your airplane's gate, wait to board (perhaps getting a coffee at a kiosk). The plane boards, and you are seated by a flight attendant and perhaps greeted by the captain. You sit in your seat, flanked on either side by other travelers. The flight taxies down the runway, lifts into the air, you rise above the clouds and then just fly. After some time, maybe an hour, maybe many, the fasten seat belts light comes on, you put your tray table in the upright position, and you glide down for a smooth landing. The plane taxies down the runway to the gate and you disembark. Another successful flight.

So, as a parent, who are you in this metaphor? Everyone.

You are responsible for every single aspect of the entire flight experience for your children. You are homeland security. You are the flight attendant, the captain, and even the mechanic that works on the airplane. You are the person who makes sure the tarmac is smooth, and ready for takeoff. You are even the seat-mate on the plane. Your presence as a parent impacts and influences every aspect of your child's life.

You can see why parenting is so hard. We need to be in so many places, doing so many different jobs in order to be successful, and our success as parents has so much to do with our kids success in life. Can kids be successful in spite of bad parenting? Absolutely. There are examples all over the place. But those are exceptions. Kids thrive when we help them to thrive, and wilt when we don't. This does not mean we have to be perfect. On the contrary, the act of striving to be the best parent possible is the most important part.

Need examples?

Kids who eat dinner with their parents are more likely to be successful in school and do well later in life. Do these parents sit around talking about the evils of universe? Do pearls of wisdom drip off their tongues or do they offer motivation that would make Vince Lombardi proud? Nope. They talk about homework. They talk about football and weather and Aunt Ida's new garden. The act of talking is the best form of prevention available to us.

There will be times for the 'evils of the universe' speech, sure. But for the most part, you simply need to be present, to be engaged.

Want another example? Do you know what one of the primary predictors of whether a teen will use and abuse alcohol? Parental attitudes and expectations. Just letting them know how you feel can be a really powerful form of protection. Again, the best thing we can do for our kids is to help them make good choices. Talk to them and connect with them, and you will be a parenting superstar.

It's not hard stuff. In fact, with Kidversation, it could not be easier. Think of us as a parenting coach. We help you find ways to connect to your kids on all the different topics where they need you most. As your partner, we teach you and guide you to be the best parent you can be, which in turn will help your kids feel safe and confident to make the best choices they can.

The Parenting Path

It is helpful to think about one of the early teachings of Buddhism. Think of tuning a guitar string — if you tighten the string too much, it snaps, and if you tighten it too little, it will not play. Kids are the same. When tuned just the right amount - music!

We need to find the middle path, the balanced path, the Parenting Path. If we put too much pressure on kids, they snap or they rebel or they become unhappy, perfectionistic zombies without learning to think for themselves. And if we expect or give too little, they will likely never realize their full potential – they might float listlessly along, and they will be susceptible to all sorts of bad outside influences.

The parenting path strikes a middle ground, where we guide them and protect them without smothering them or denying them the chance to think and grow for themselves.

Again, simplicity rules. By working your way through Kidversation, the Parenting Path will become clear. By sharing and listening, you show your kids you can offer guidance while at the same time respecting what they have to say. They will appreciate your balance of compassion and empathy with your willingness to be the parent.

A Not-So-Little Secret

Here is the one not-so-little secret that can mean all the difference in your relationship with your children - they WANT to talk to you. They want to share the details of their lives with you. They want to confide in you and have you give them guidance and love as only a parent can.

And here is a fact that is not much of a secret. Kids are lousy at letting us know how much they need us. They are almost purely ego driven (in the simplest terms, their minds are almost only capable of seeing the world in terms of themselves). Even through high school, they tend to think about the world concretely - they see things as absolutes with little room for flexibility…black and white. And many live at the extremes of emotion - they are either overly emotional and reactive or they are flat and not emotional at all.

When taken together (ego-driven, concrete thinker, emotional extremes), a question like "how was your day?" can be a minefield - one wrong step and kaboom!

There is a giant canyon between the little secret that your kids want to talk to you and the not-much-of-a-secret that they can be lousy at talking to you. This canyon is what separates so many kids from really confiding in their parents, from really communicating what they are thinking and how they are feeling. Kidversation bridges this chasm. How? By giving you the tools you need to give your kids something they yearn for - guidance. So dive into Kidversation headfirst. Read the additional parenting advice. And start having fun engaging your kids in deep and heartfelt conversation. Their 'not-so-little-secret' will become apparent to you soon enough.

Additional Parenting Advice

The goal of Kidversation is to make your conversations as productive, enjoyable and beneficial as possible. The pages that follow will give you some additional tools and guidance. By using these tips and tricks, you will be able to maximize the joy and benefits of each conversation.

Our first and most important advice is this: when working through the questions with your kids, listen closely and actively with an open heart and open mind.

This is the mantra of Kidversation - keep an open heart and open mind. We spend too much time trying to live up to some ideal of parenting that says we have to solve our children's problems for them or we have to be their best friends or we have to break the bank buying them stuff. The thing is, kids just want to be heard. And as parents, one of the greatest gifts in the world we can give them is ourselves, our attention, our focus. If you need a saying to help you remember this, how about:

"Being present is the best present I can give my kids."

Corny? Maybe. But true and crucial and so powerful nonetheless.

With that, here is some additional advice to help you in your discussions:

Your children's emotions are twisted up like vines

Talking about happy or fun times can be really close to sad or hard times for a child (especially teens) - happiness and sadness, love and hate, joy and rage all are so closely related. This is because feeling one emotion opens us up to the opposite, like a swinging pendulum. Discussing this will let your child know that you understand the tension they might be feeling, even if they do not yet understand this for themselves. You will hear this idea played out as you go through many different cards.

Turn off the Parental Filter

As much as anything, Kidversation is an exercise in listening quietly and patiently. The goal is to listen without bias, without the parental filter that says "this is acceptable" or "what the heck were you thinking?" The goal is to build (or rebuild) trust. When you start editorializing or sounding off on their answers, you are taking away trust. And this advice goes far beyond Kidversation. We need to be able to really listen closely to our children if we are to bridge the chasm that sometimes can form between us. Remember, kids want to be heard. Just being present goes a long way.

Look for Teacheable Moments

An obvious opportunity for this is including lessons you've learned over your life while answering thes questions. But other teachable moments include how to have fun, how to be silly, how to listen and watch and learn - the list goes on and on. Ultimately, our every choice, word and action teaches, intentional or not. The goal is to understand WHAT we are teaching, how we are doing it, and what we would rather teach instead.

Always be engaged with your kids

You really only lose with your children when you do not engage with them in a trusting and loving way. And once you stop engaging with them, turning this around can be hard. As the parent, the goal is therefore to stay engaged on an ongoing basis. Keep going back time and again to learn more, to be a part of their lives. You might be made uncomfortable, you might even hear them curse you and get angry at you. They need to get used to you injecting yourself into the seemingly boring details of their life. But if you stay engaged and eventually they will come around. And remember, you are there to listen and process, not necessarily to condone or condemn.

Show you are a real person

Your children need to see you as a person, someone with strengths and flaws. You need to be the parent, but you need to be a real person to them as well. By showing them your full humanity, you accomplish a couple things. First, they can have more realistic expectations of you. When you fail them, and we all do eventually, you can focus your energy on making things better for next time. This is far more productive than trying to rebuild the shattered illusion that you are perfect. And second, it is easier to listen to, and learn from, real people. The more our kids identify with us, the easier it is for them to learn from us.

Set realistic expectations

This goes along with the previous point. The importance of realistic expectations can't be overemphasized. If your kids see you as someone with your good parts and your bad parts, but someone who consistently tries, then they can start to have those same expectations for themselves. Kids who expect too little from themselves never quite realize their potential. And kids who are overzealous perfectionists struggle to celebrate their success. They rarely feel the internal sense that they are wonderful, beautiful people, regardless of how successful they might be.

Help them to know that their feelings are normal

Kids are growing in so many ways - physically, intellectually and emotionally. As a result, they often struggle to understand if these changes are normal and they want to understand if their thoughts and feelings make them different. We don't want our kids to feel like they are necessarily the same as everyone else, that they are not unique. At the same time, you need to help them see that most of what they are feeling and experiencing is not just normal, but is shared by many others. As you direct the conversation through answering the guiding questions for yourself, you will be doing just that.

Good parenting is a practice, one that must be done with compassion for yourself and your kids

If you are familiar at all with yoga, you understand this sense of creating a Practice. Or if it helps, think of learning to play piano. We obviously don't sit down our first time at the piano and bang out Chopin. Chopsticks, maybe. The time, the space, the work between first playing Chopsticks and finally playing Chopin is the Practice. We need to do the same thing with parenting. Learning to react appropriately and calmly when your kids make you want to scream, rant and rave is a Practice. Showing love and compassion when anger and frustration are so much easier is a Practice. Learning to ask your kids the right questions, and then learning to listen with an open heart and open mind is absolutely a Practice.

Here is a hint to make it successful. When learning to play piano, the person who gets so frustrated that he walks away will likely never make it to Chopin. We all make mistakes. Part of our Practice as parents is learning to accept our mistakes calmly and to learn what went right and what went wrong so we can either duplicate or avoid as the case may be. This is one of the main reasons for the Debrief Questions.

We learn best when we are part of a feedback loop

This goes along with the previous point. If you make your parenting a Practice, the best way to do so is to sit down after connecting with your kids (good or bad) to think about what went right and what went wrong. The best parents in the world still mess up on occasion. We yell when calm would be more useful. We criticize when compassion is needed. We say and do things that, if observing ourselves from the outside, would cause us to feel embarassed or ashamed. The best way to deal with these mistakes is to learn from them and work on strategies to keep from repeating them.

The best teaching comes from a light hand

Sharing a story with real thought and emotion is far more powerful than trying to beat a lesson in through mindless repetition. Perhaps it will help to think about it this way: parent as though you were parenting yourself. Would you want someone in your face repeating the same idea over and over? Or would you want to learn the lesson in a meaningful and memorable way, one that lasts?

Give your kids a chance to listen to you and learn from you. But do so with patience, understanding and love. It will probably take a while for what you are sharing to settle in. But don't ever forget - they are listening and learning. Stay calm and consistent and have faith that your light handed approach is working.

There is little long-term value in getting angry

Anger is usually for the parent, not the kids. Getting mad rarely ends the problematic behavior in the long-term. Rather than punishment, natural consequences are truly the most effective way to teach and end the problems. If you catch your child lying, yelling at them and sending them to their room is far less effective than talking to them about why lying is wrong, what problems come from lying, and then guiding them to find a natural consequence (apologizing, telling the truth, losing a trust-based priviledge). When your kids do something inappropriate or wrong, rather than getting angry, use it as an opportunity to fix the behavior. It is not a question of letting them 'get away' with something, but rather moving them gradually to a place where they do not do it in the firstplace.

One last point. There are definitely times when getting angry is absolutely the right thing to do. The occasions where you do get angry are all the more powerful for being rare. They will know they've done something really wrong this way.

Be prepared to get more help

If you hear anything at any point that you think means bigger problems, look into counseling or other help for yourself and your child. There is no shame in taking the steps necessary to help your child to start healing. If you ignore problems, they do not go away, they just get buried to be dealt with another day, most likely causing additional damage. And if you are scared that getting help will break the trust you are building, you need to weigh the cost of not acting. It may take time to help them understand why you acted. They might be really angry and feel betrayed initially. But if you let them know that your job as the parent is to keep them safe, then they should hopefully come to understand over time.

Communication and connection are habits

It is crucial to talk with your kids about the most mundane and boring of things. For example - how was school, what did you think of dinner, tell me about the movie you saw, etc.. By showing a deep and loving interest in every part of their life, you are taking a big step forward - things that seem small and trivial to you are probably huge and important to them.

It really is true that the more you talk, the more you talk. If you need a metaphor to help, think of it like taming a wild animal. Rush it, and they run away and you lose out. But take it slowly and you will eventually be rewarded (hopefully without the scratches and teeth marks.)

Things create/perpetuate themselves. Do your best to show them the right behaviors.

Anger in you creates anger in your kids. Lying creates lying. Rewarding tantrums creates tantrums to get what they want. Everything we do, our attitudes, behaviors and choices, teaches our kids. Need an example? If you smoke, your kids are far more likely to smoke when they become teens or adults. Even if you tell your kids over and over that they should never smoke. Even if they tell you over and over how much they hate the very sight of cigarettes when they are younger. Seeing you smoke is a far more powerful teacher than words can ever convey.

The problem is, we can't be perfect. We all say and do things we wish we could take back. If you struggle with this, admitting so to your kids is a good step. You are modeling humility and a willingness to admit mistakes and an ability to learn. Remember, everything we do teaches our children, for better or worse. And never stop trying to improve these problems in yourself. That is also a powerful teacher for your kids.

Use honesty well and for the right reasons

Your kids will trust you when you trust them. Don't use honesty as a weapon to force them to open up. Don't manipulate them by saying "I told you the truth, now you have to tell me the truth." And don't treat your kids like a confession booth. They are your children, so everthing you tell them should have a larger reason or purpose behind it. Think about why you are sharing information and how it will help them. Don't look to them for absolution for your problems. It is not their job to make you feel better. You need to seek that out on your own. You need to tell them the truth, but focus on making it an age appropriate teaching tool for them, not for you.

Parent in a mirror

It is hard to understand your kids until you understand yourself. You need to look at yourself first, your own attitudes, ideas, and choices before you can really understand how you are impacting your children. Do you react in anger most of the time? Do you ignore problems till they get out of control? Do you try to be pals with your kid instead of the parent? Until you know yourself, it is hard to determine what changes you need to make. So start with a mirror. And if you do struggle with this, be open and honest with your kids about your struggle, and what you are doing about it.

Offer internalized 'I' responses instead of judgment

People (kids definitely included) tend to get defensive and to shut down when they feel judged. Kids often need help feeling that their attitudes, perceptions, and beliefs are acceptable. It can help to tell them how you would feel if something that they did or something that happened to them happened to you. For example, "If my best friend said she hated me, I would feel pretty upset." or "I understand wanting to hit someone who yelled in my face. I would struggle to make the right choice too." It should not sound like you are judging. This will let your kids feel safer listening and hopefully encouraging them to share in turn. Don't make it patronizing or condescending. This is an opportunity to teach them about healthy emotional responses. And if your kids are older, don't be surprised if they get angry or frustrated. If what you say makes them feel bad, they might lash out at you. Don't take it personally and stay calm. It means you are getting somewhere.

INSTRUCTIONS

It might seem a bit silly to have instructions for conversation questions, right? Just sit down and talk. And that might be all it takes for you. However, if you have struggled at all to connect with your kids in the past, and then you sit down, pull out a deck of cards, and say "time to talk!" you might not get the reaction you are looking for. With this in mind, we offer the following:

General Guidelines

We designed the Kidversation cards to make getting started as easy as possible.

- Pick a question - either pick a random question or have a planned approach.

- Read the questions for parents to answer and think about how your own answers and insight can help guide and frame the conversation.

- Have the conversation!

- Finally, fill out the Debrief Questions. These include "What went well?" "What needs work?" and assigning a rating to the conversation (where 5 means 'Great' and 1 means 'Poor').

A quick note on the debrief questions. Filling these out is important for a few reasons.

- First, doing so will give you a record of your conversation, something you can look back on later.

- Second, by thinking about the conversation for a bit afterwards, you will have a chance to reflect on what went well and what you need to work on for the next conversation. Remember, Kidversation has two primary goals: help you build a stronger connection with your kids AND help you to strengthen your parenting. The debrief questions help in achieving both goals.

- And third, one of the recommended strategies is that you return to topics as your kids age. If you have a record of the first conversation, you have something to compare with later conversations. This will help you in thinking about what went better, where has there been improvement, and what has changed over time. The rating in particular makes you really decide how well or poorly you think it went. Be honest, and don't feel bad if you think things are going poorly. Use the "What needs work" question to think about how you can be constantly improving.

Additional Strategies

As we said, the guidelines are straightforward.

1. Pick the right question, do a little preparation.

2. Have the conversation

3. Spend a few more minutes doing the debrief questions.

Depending on the relationship you already have in place with your kids, you might need to help ease them into fully using Kidversation successfully. With that in mind, we would like to offer some additional strategies. Pick and choose to meet your needs.

Listen with an open heart and an open mind

This might be the single most important advice we can give you. It is so important, we also discuss it in the introduction. You need to be able to listen to your kids without judgment, without bias, and with a sincere desire to hear what they have to say. Your trust and your openness will be paid back with trust and with openness. Remember, they want to share with you – you just need to make it as easy as possible for them to do so.

Begin with picking one of the lighter questions

If you start with one of the heavier or more personal questions, it might be a bit overwhelming, so proceed with caution. As your conversations become more regular, start asking the kids if they are ready to move into the more challenging questions. Give them the choice and let them guide you. Do not try taking them anywhere they do not want to or are not ready to go.

Explain to them why you want to do the questions

If it will help, tell them it is about you and not them, something like "I feel like I need a bit of help with this. I want to learn, and this seems like a fun way to talk more. Let's give a few questions a try and see how it goes." Check your ego at the door. Just because YOU want to do these questions, that might not necessarily mean THEY are ready to do so. Helping them to understand that you will take it slowly, one question at a time, should help ease them in.

For younger kids, make a game out of it

Preselect questions that you think will work well for your kids. Then have them pick a question from the ones you selected. If they really need motivation to get started, take the game further by making it a guessing game, where you try and guess what their answer is going to be. You should only take this path if they need a bit of encouragement to get started, and keep it really lighthearted. Also keep in mind that teens will discuss things in a different way than younger children.

Read their reactions and react accordingly

Listen for cues that they are uncomfortable or do not want to talk about a topic and then drop it for the time being. Unless you think it is an urgent matter or an issue of safety, don't push. Rather, give the topic a break for a while (days or weeks), then come back to it a different way. Something like "I noticed when we talked about [topic], you seemed to be pretty upset/ frustrated/angry. I don't want to push, but I think we should talk about this a More." Keep softening the sell (using less and less pressure) till you can get them to open up on their own about this. If it is neither urgent nor dangerous, time can be your friend here.

Be careful when using humor

It is a strange and unfortunate fact that while adults often use humor to relieve tension, kids (especially if they are feeling any tension) often react to humor like they were scalded with burning hot water. They tend to be concrete thinkers and don't always get our humor. The goal is to get them to open up – not shut them down with a poorly placed joke or teasing (no matter how gentle you think it is). If you think it will help, promise them you will not make any jokes – and then stick to it. Otherwise you risk breaking trust.

Turn off the Parent Filter

Commit to them that you will turn off the parent filter unless you hear something that you have to act on. Let them know that you want to listen and share your own stories. More on the parent filter in the introduction.

Be honest

Commit to them that you will be honest. You will share with them your own stories, your own experiences, and you will only hold back things that you can't share for one reason or another (you can't break someone else's trust, they are not mature enough to hear the details, etc.) And then follow through. The purpose of the cards is to open the connection between you and your kids. Lying short-circuits this goal, so don't do it. This is especially important if you have a history of problems or trust issues with your kids.

For the more challenging Teen-only cards, this can be especially challenging. You need to use your discretion as to what you share and do not share. Holding back is different than outright lying. But keep in mind, kids know more than we ever think they know. If we think we are holding back to protect them, odds are, they are already hearing it from somewhere else.

As discussed in the introduction, don't use your kids as a confession booth. Your first priority should be ensuring that what you share with your kids is teaching the lesson you intended.

Be a vault for whatever they tell you

Assure them that, unless you talk about it first, you will keep whatever they confide in you to yourself. However, remind them that the exception is if you hear something that you have to act on, especially if it is a matter of safety. Otherwise, you are a vault, a veritable lockbox – and if you slip up and do break their trust, you will have to work twice as hard to earn it back.

Build The Conversation Patiently

Especially if you feel like you've lost connection with your children, don't expect trumpets to blare and angels to descend because you are making an effort - and don't expect your kids to just jump right in gladly. The idea is to build up conversation as slowly as it takes to make it work. You have all the patience you need - especially if you keep the one main secret in mind -

your kids want to talk to you. They might not admit it. They might even deny it at length. But if you take it slowly, and are open and honest about your sincere desire to make this work, they should come around sooner rather than later. If things are really strained and you are not sure how to get things started, here is a suggested script. "I know we've had problems talking in the past. I'm sorry - and I want to try again. I got Kidversation as a way to help us get the conversation started. We can take small steps, but I really want to try." You will be amazed at the power of a sustained and hearfelt effort has in rebuilding trust.

Make the Conversations Age Appropriate

With the exception of the questions clearly labeled Teen, all the questions can be made age appropriate for all but the youngest children. Adapt and adjust the topic so that you are meeting your child at his or her level without forcing them to a place where they are uncomfortable. And as your kids get older, it will be fascinating and useful to try some questions again with them to see how their answers change over time.

Share the good, the bad, and the ugly

This goes along with the prior point. You obviously need to keep things appropriate for kids, but as much as possible, don't lie to them. There are many reasons for this. They need to know their legacy. If you are not telling them things to protect them from some family secret, you are denying them the chance to cope in a healthy way. And if you think they are better off not knowing about something (for example talking about sex or drugs to middle schoolers and older), you are denying the hard reality that they will learn it anyway - at school, on the bus, somewhere else and from far less trustworthy and reliable sources than yourself. Obviously, their age matters here. And if you know your kids can't handle something, you need to meet them where they are. But in the long run, denying the truth is a bad strategy.

Kidversation Questions

The goal of Kidversation is to make sure you and your family get as much as possible out of the discussion. To help you along, each Kidversation question has 4 parts:

1. The Question - right at the top of the page and clearly underlined. There are also additional questions to keep the conversation going.

2. Discussion Guide - this contains questions and ideas you can use to talk about your own experiences, which will help you guide the discussion.

3. Parent-to-Parent - this contains some additional details, background information and other bits that will help as you talk. You do NOT have to share this information with your child if you do not want to, though in many cases it makes sense to do so.

4. Debrief Questions - once you are done with the conversation, use this space to take notes and answer some questions on what went well, what can be improved on for next time, and anything you want to remember for the future.

Remember, Kidversation will help you connect you to your kids and to improve the types of choices you make as a parent. By using ALL of the tools listed above, you will be taking every step possible towards doing so. Good luck and have fun!

Beliefs

What does faith mean to you?

Question type: **Beliefs**

How can you guide the discussion?
What do you believe in? When has faith played an important part in your life? Have you ever been troubled by your faith? It is important for your kids to understand the full journey you've taken with your faith, the good and the bad. You can help to normalize any questions or doubts they have, and be a source of help and comfort.

Parent-to-parent...More insight
So much of what we know and think regarding faith comes from family. But like all other things, children have a way of developing their own definitions and understanding of what faith means. Give them space and let them work through this. Be prepared to share openly (and without judgment) your perspective on your own faith. And if your kids believe in something you do not, try and resist the temptation to push them too hard. That is a good way to push them away. Rather, keep an open and honest dialogue going, share and listen, and be as open as possible to their point of view. Faith can be a great way to grow together, so don't let differing views pull you apart. Keep your heart and mind open.

Supporting Questions

- Do you feel like your beliefs match mine? How about the rest of the family?

- Do you ever talk about faith with your friends?

- What does it mean to respect other faiths?

How did the conversation go?

Great		Fair		Poor
5	4	3	2	1

What went well?

_____

_____

What needs work?

_____

_____

What surprised you?

_____

_____

The next time you do a Kidversation question, what do you want to do differently?

_____

_____

What does leadership mean to you?

Question type: **Beliefs**

> **How can you guide the discussion?**
> How do you feel about your own leadership ability? Do you feel more comfortable leading the charge or letting someone else lead. Talking to your kids is a great opportunity for self-examination. If you want to become more of a leader, talk about why and what doing so means to you.

Parent-to-parent...More insight

Kids see leaders and followers every day - in school, on the playground, in sports, in the home. Do they see themselves as leaders or followers? What qualities do they see in a leader? Help them to understand that some people feel more comfortable taking charge, but that good leadership means being fair and responsible. And help them to think about quiet kinds of leadership such as not going along with something their friends are doing if they do not think it is right. This kind of moral leadership is just as important (arguably more so) than more visible forms.

Supporting Questions
- Do you think you are a natural leader?

- How do you feel when you see your friends leading, instead of you?

- What kind of responsibilities come with leadership?

How did the conversation go?

Great		Fair		Poor
5	4	3	2	1

What went well?

_____

_____

What needs work?

_____

_____

What surprised you?

_____

_____

The next time you do a Kidversation question, what do you want to do differently?

_____

_____

What does equality mean to you?

Question type: **Beliefs**

How can you guide the discussion?
Question your own beliefs about this important concept. In a society that is largely defined by equality, how close are we to attaining this ideal? Does President Obama change things? Have you had your own experiences with discrimination or other unfair treatment? Share (appropriately) how this made you feel, and how you overcame it. You can help to normalize your kids own experiences, and make them more likely to open up.

Parent-to-parent...More insight
Concepts such as equality are defined and redefined by kids at different stages in their lives. As concrete thinkers, younger kids might think about everyone getting the same - they don't tend to understand the larger concept of discrimination. As they get older, kids start to understand the larger societal implications of this concept. Kids will most likely have questions about racism, discrimination and other unfair treatment. Listen and share honestly. You might hear things that trigger your parent filter such as attitudes or beliefs you disagree with. Rather than 'jumping on' them, take a step back and listen for the roots of those beliefs. Talk through it and see where you can get THEM to connect the dots rather than doing it for them.

Supporting Questions
- Have you ever been the victim of inequality?

- Do you ever see inequality in school? At home?

- If you could do one thing to get others to think about treating everyone equally, what would it be?

How did the conversation go?

Great		Fair		Poor
5	4	3	2	1

What went well?

_____

_____

What needs work?

_____

_____

What surprised you?

_____

_____

The next time you do a Kidversation question, what do you want to do differently?

_____

_____

What does justice mean to you?

Question type: **Beliefs**

How can you guide the discussion?
What do you think of our legal system? What about punishment? Redemption? Help your kids to understand why you hold certain attitudes. Where do they come from? Do you see any of these same attitudes in your children? Sharing a little indignation now and then can show them your righteous side.

Parent-to-parent...More insight
To build hope in the future, kids need to understand what justice means in our country. If you are not familiar with our legal system, this is a great topic you can explore together. Our society has not always been just, but has almost always aspired to it. For example, we are governed by the rule of law. This plays out in our everyday lives in countless ways (product safety laws, civil rights laws, mandatory schooling laws). Work with your kids to research this together. Start with http://bensguide.gpo.gov/ for age specific information on our government.

Supporting Questions
- Can you think of a time when you saw someone who was treated unjustly?

- What do you know about our legal system?

- Would you ever want to be a lawyer or police officer? Why?

How did the conversation go?

Great		Fair		Poor
5	4	3	2	1

What went well?

_____

_____

What needs work?

_____

_____

What surprised you?

_____

_____

The next time you do a Kidversation question, what do you want to do differently?

_____

_____

What does fairness mean to you?

Question type: **Beliefs**

How can you guide the discussion?
Do you remember the first time you felt life was unfair? Or the first time your parent's broke a commitment? Or perhaps a time when feeling things were unfair really made a big impression on you. We often develop our sense of fairness at a young age. Share your memories with your kids, and also examine if you are holding onto any ideas around this carried over from your childhood. Help your kids to understand how we are always growing and changing.

Parent-to-parent...More insight
They say 'That isn't fair!' - we respond 'Life isn't fair!' It is such an easy response. But is it a good response, a kind response, one that respects the true sadness a child feels when they think they have been treated unfairly? Not really. We need to hear everything our kids say with an open mind and an open heart. If you think life is unfair, the question you should next answer with your child is 'How do we work to make it fair?' And rather than thinking life is unfair, think about how ideas of fairness come from within - 'Life is unfair because of what happened to me.' Rather, think about how life is neither fair nor unfair - life just is. We largely define fairness for ourselves. And we are therefore responsible for how we react to and deal when faced with such challenging situations.

Supporting Questions
- Do you think you are usually treated fairly by me? Other family members? Your teachers? Friends?

- Have you ever tried to help out when you saw someone else being treated unfairly?

How did the conversation go?

Great		Fair		Poor
5	4	3	2	1

What went well?

_____

_____

What needs work?

_____

_____

What surprised you?

_____

_____

The next time you do a Kidversation question, what do you want to do differently?

_____

_____

What does peace mean to you? What does war mean?

Question type: **Beliefs**

> **How can you guide the discussion?**
> War can divide a country, family, or friends. Has this ever happened to you? Our country has been at war at least once every decade in the recent past. How has this effected you? Share your perspective on war and peace with your kids, and then listen to their perspective. Listen with compassion and be ready to explore this topic further, especially if you hear any fear or concern.

Parent-to-parent...More insight

At a time of war (or when war is in the recent past), it is hard to think what peace means to us. What does it mean to have peace at home while our country fights wars thousands of miles away? What about living in a neighborhood where gangs are fighting outside? Kids want to feel safe at any age, but as they get older, they also need to understand the world around them. As a parent, it can be terribly difficult to balance giving them information to help them be informed citizens while at the same time wanting to protect them. In finding this balance, you are giving your kids great tools to move into later stages of life. A great place to start is the newspaper. Pick stories that show the many parts of war (soldiers being hurt or killed, the struggles of families, soldiers helping civilians, etc.) and then discuss how things could be turned around if peace were the goal.

Supporting Questions
- What do you think it would be like to be in the middle of war as a soldier or a civilian?

- What are some things you can do to be a peacemaker amongst your friends and at school?

How did the conversation go?

Great		Fair		Poor
5	4	3	2	1

What went well?

_____

_____

What needs work?

_____

_____

What surprised you?

_____

_____

The next time you do a Kidversation question, what do you want to do differently?

_____

_____

Can you learn from watching others, or do you need to make the mistakes yourself?

Question type: **Beliefs**

How can you guide the discussion?
What life lesson did you learn by watching others? Did your parents try and teach you these lessons, but you ignored them? And if so, what were the consequences? Use your own experiences to show the kids the mistakes you (or others you know of) could have avoided by learning rather than doing. Don't be heavy handed in doing so - the goal should be modeling right behavior.

Parent-to-parent...More insight
Sharing your own life experiences can help your kids to learn and grow without repeating your mistakes. But using 1 liners - 'Don't do drugs' - ignores their need for deeper understanding. And kids tend to seek experiences, rather than learning from words. If you don't want them to actually make these mistakes, you need to connect with them on the reasons why the mistake is not worth the experience. And if they see that you can listen with compassion, they are more likely to come to you to share thoughts on actions not yet taken, actions that might lead to mistakes. In other words, sometimes the best way to make them listen is to say as little as possible.

Supporting Questions
- Tell me about a time you avoided a mistake by seeing someone else make it?

- Tell me about a time when you could have avoided a mistake but made it anyway?

How did the conversation go?

	Great		Fair		Poor
	5	4	3	2	1

What went well?

_____

_____

What needs work?

_____

_____

What surprised you?

_____

_____

The next time you do a Kidversation question, what do you want to do differently?

_____

_____

Emotional

Have you ever been depressed?

Question type: **Emotional**

How can you guide the discussion?

Talk about times you or other family members have been depressed. You can help your child to understand that everyone gets sad and many get depressed. If you have your own experience with this, it might be scary to share, but it is the right thing to do for two reasons: depression can be genetic, so they need to know their legacy; and hearing your story will help connect them to you and will normalize their own experiences.

Parent-to-parent...More insight

At least 10% of all people get seriously depressed. For most people, sadness comes and goes. Clinical depression is different. If the depression hits hard and often, maybe it is time to get help. There is a line between typical teen angst and real, medical depression. If you have any questions about this for your child, it is time to consult a professional. One thing to be aware of: if your child is depressed, trust will be hard to come by and easily broken. Be as honest and open as is reasonable and know that there might be a short-term breakdown of their trust for you, but when safety is involved, it is still something you must do.

Supporting Questions
- What do you think the difference is between sadness and depression?

- What are a few ways being sad is good for you?

- What are some things you do to feel better after feeling sad or depressed?

How did the conversation go?

	Great		Fair		Poor
	5	4	3	2	1

What went well?

_____

_____

What needs work?

_____

_____

What surprised you?

_____

_____

The next time you do a Kidversation question, what do you want to do differently?

_____

_____

Have any of your friends ever talked about being depressed?

Question type: **Emotional**

How can you guide the discussion?
Talk about experiences you've had with friends who have been depressed. How did it make you feel to see someone spiraling downward without being able to help? Convey your understanding of this sense of powerlessness, help them to see you as someone who has been there. And if they talk about sadness instead of depression, that is fine. Labels matter less than understanding their experiences.

Parent-to-parent...More insight
Depression is a painful reality for kids. It can make it hard to stay friends with people and it can lead to other problems like using alcohol, drugs, and even cutting (self injury with a blade) to "self-medicate." If your kids show any anxiety about seeing depression in their friends, let them know it is OK to talk to school counselors to get help. Sadness is normal. Let them know that for many kids whose emotions are growing as fast as their bodies, minor bouts of sadness or depression are normal, but that they need to be on the lookout for signs that it is turning to something worse. With open lines of communication, you can be a source of information and support for your kids on this painful but ever present subject.

Supporting Questions
- If you thought one of your friends was seriously depressed, what would you do? Where would you go for help?

- What do you think causes depression? What causes sadness? What is the difference between the two?

How did the conversation go?

Great		Fair		Poor
5	4	3	2	1

What went well?

_____

_____

What needs work?

_____

_____

What surprised you?

_____

_____

The next time you do a Kidversation question, what do you want to do differently?

_____

_____

If you could change any one part about your childhood, what would it be?

Question type: **Emotional**

How can you guide the discussion?
Talk about one of your own challenging or difficult parts of childhood. They will benefit from your own struggles and challenges. Or perhaps you wish you'd taken a chance or risk that you were too scared to attempt at the time. Involve your kids in your self-reflection, then brainstorm one or two ways to start addressing what you see as a shortcoming. And remember, it is never too late to learn to play!

Parent-to-parent...More insight
Few people have what anyone would identify as an ideal childhood. Even people that seem like they had it all feel there were parts of their childhood that were hard. In addition, fear keeps many kids from trying things they might have otherwise wanted to do. Ultimately, you should help your kids to understand that it is never too late to start working towards the things we want. The opportunity to change is always with us. And don't be surprised if your kids talk about wanting a bigger room or better clothes. You can help steer this discussion to bigger ideas if you want, but know that kids are really concrete and feel pressure to fit in strongly. And remember, don't feel hurt or take it personally. This is a time for you to learn, not judge.

Supporting Questions
- What can I do to help you make this change?

- What have been your favorite parts of your childhood so far?

- Are there any other things you might want to change if you could?

How did the conversation go?

Great		Fair		Poor
5	4	3	2	1

What went well?

_____

_____

What needs work?

_____

_____

What surprised you?

_____

_____

The next time you do a Kidversation question, what do you want to do differently?

_____

_____

Do you feel like I support you emotionally?

Question type: **Emotional**

> **How can you guide the discussion?**
> Did you feel emotionally supported by your parents? If not, what negative patterns are you re-living from your childhood? We tend to parent the way we were parented. Do you notice any patterns that tend to come out, especially when you are around family. Help your kids to feel safe sharing their insights about how you might be carrying parts of your childhood with you.

Parent-to-parent...More insight
This is a hard one. Feeling slighted is a full time job for many kids. If they feel supported, can they help you to understand why? If not, do not get sad or angry. Kids tend to overstate things, so revisit this topic again when they are in a different mood. And if they truly do not feel supported, explore what they are looking for - what they need to feel emotional support. Ask how you can support them better and then set specific goals (e.g. 'We will discuss how you are doing every day after school and you will answer honestly.') And perhaps, the problem is no fault of your own. If they want things you can't provide them (e.g. 'I would feel more supported if you bought me a sports car'), explain your reasons why and see if you can find a balanced, healthy middle ground.

Supporting Questions
- Is this answer always the same, or does it change depending on how things are going?

- Why do you think it is important for parents to support their kids emotionally?

- Should kids support their parents emotionally?

How did the conversation go?

Great		Fair		Poor
5	4	3	2	1

What went well?

_____

_____

What needs work?

_____

_____

What surprised you?

_____

_____

The next time you do a Kidversation question, what do you want to do differently?

_____

_____

What do I do that upsets or scares you the most?

Question type: **Emotional**

How can you guide the discussion?
What did your parents do that upset you. Share your own turmoil - the things that happened in your childhood that scared you. Often these can be memories we've pushed down. But it is very much possible that you are repeating with your kids the same things that scared you - something you should put an end to as quickly as possible - start by discussing alternative behaviors.

Parent-to-parent...More insight
This might be really tough for you - it can break our hearts to have to confront what we do that scares our children, but it will help to get things out there. Often it is what we do not know that makes everything hardest. And if you ask this question again another week (or even another day), the answer might be different. Kids are like that. Still, no parent wants to be the source of their children's fears. Part of your job is to be the source of their comfort and safety.

Supporting Questions
- Does it feel like the things I do that scare you are more often intentional or unintentional?

- What do you think I can do differently so that I don't scare or upset you this way anymore?

How did the conversation go?

Great		Fair		Poor
5	4	3	2	1

What went well?

_____

_____

What needs work?

_____

_____

What surprised you?

_____

_____

The next time you do a Kidversation question, what do you want to do differently?

_____

_____

Outside of our family, who do you turn to for emotional support?

Question type: **Emotional**

How can you guide the discussion?
Did you have friends or neighbors, or perhaps a coach or teacher who you turned to for help? By sharing your stories about seeking help outside the family, you can help your kids to understand that doing so is OK. But also let them know that you also need to know about important details - that is part of building trust.

Parent-to-parent...More insight
Especially for older kids, they often turn to others outside the family for support. You need to know as much as you can about who these people are so you can help your child to understand the advice they get. Kids who feel so terribly misunderstood (and what kid does not) can easily fall prey to negative outside influences and even to those seeking to take advantage. You need to balance giving your kids the space they need with keeping them safe - and helping them to understand the difference.

Supporting Questions
- Why do you think it is important to have other people (outside our immediate family) who support you emotionally?

- Are there other people like friends or others who you feel you support emotionally? Why?

How did the conversation go?

Great		Fair		Poor
5	4	3	2	1

What went well?

_____

_____

What needs work?

_____

_____

What surprised you?

_____

_____

The next time you do a Kidversation question, what do you want to do differently?

_____

_____

What is the hardest part about being a guy and what is the hardest part about being a girl?

Question type: **Emotional**

How can you guide the discussion?
Ideas about gender come from many places - childhood, social attitudes, personal biases. Where do your beliefs come from? Have you ever questioned your ideas about gender (what it means to be a guy or girl)? Have any of your biases or attitudes made it to your kids? If you or your kids feel you need to adjust your thoughts on this, have them help you to brainstorm ways to do so.

Parent-to-parent...More insight
Gender matters to kids. Younger kids often group themselves by boys and girls. And as kids get older, they develop biases and stereotypes. If they got these from you or others in your family, it is time to hit the reset button. Gender stereotyping is painful and limiting. You need to be working to help your kids be the best at whatever they want to do. Now help them to understand why a 'level playing field' is best for all people. And if they see sexism or discrimination in those around them, help them to feel more comfortable calling these out for what they really are - just plain wrong.

Supporting Questions
- What is the easiest part about being a guy? A girl?

- Do you think it is true that there are 'guy' and 'girl' things (e.g. sports, fashion, games), or do think guys and girls should be able to do similar things?

How did the conversation go?

Great		Fair		Poor
5	4	3	2	1

What went well?

_____

_____

What needs work?

_____

_____

What surprised you?

_____

_____

The next time you do a Kidversation question, what do you want to do differently?

_____

_____

Describe a time when you were teased.

Question type: **Emotional**

How can you guide the discussion?

Were you teased as a child? Why? What can you share about your own experiences? Do you carry scars from your own experiences with being teased? Work with your kids to identify steps you can take to start healing. After all, words really CAN hurt worse than sticks and stones. Many scars on the outside heal much faster than the ones on the inside.

Parent-to-parent...More insight

Teasing hurts. It is one of the ways bullying starts. And it is often portrayed as humor when it is not funny. Telling your child to tough it out, or to give as much as he/she gets ignores the pain it causes and can bring on new problems. We can carry the pain of being teased, of being excluded and made to feel different, long after. If you want your kids to grow into healthy, intelligent, well adjusted people, they need to feel safe being themselves. If they are scared of teasing, this can be a real limitation for them.

Supporting Questions
- How does it feel to be teased?

- Is all teasing bad or hurtful, or is any type of teasing ever OK?

- Who does teasing hurt more, the person being teased or the person doing the teasing?
  (HINT: BOTH IN DIFFERENT WAYS)

How did the conversation go?

Great		Fair		Poor
5	4	3	2	1

What went well?

_____

_____

What needs work?

_____

_____

What surprised you?

_____

_____

The next time you do a Kidversation question, what do you want to do differently?

_____

_____

Is there anyone who've you've ever really teased? How does that make you feel?

Question type: **Emotional**

How can you guide the discussion?

Look at yourself honestly – do you tease or use abrasive humor to make your point with your kids? Your spouse? Did you tease others as a child? We teach with our actions. It is never too late to fix this - talk to your kids about where your teasing/getting teased comes from and have the kids remind you when they see it happening. You might not even know you're doing it!

Parent-to-parent...More insight

Kids tease to separate out differences. They might feel sad or angry or self-conscious, and so they lash out at others. And they might think it is funny without really intending to hurt people's feelings. Help them to understand how it makes others feel. Teach that getting teased is not an excuse to tease. And as kids move to middle and high school, teasing can quickly become an outlet for meanness and cruelty. If your child is on either end of this level of teasing, you need to intervene immediately. Both hurting and being hurt have long-term consequences that you need to address immediately. Work with your child to find the root causes is a first step. And don't forget, digital teasing (through texting, email, social networks, etc.) hurts just as much and can spread farther and faster than 'school yard' teasing. Go to stopbullying.gov to learn more.

Supporting Questions
- Can you remember why you teased him/her?

- Did you ever make amends with the person? If yes, how did it feel? If not, why not? Can you still do so?

How did the conversation go?

Great		Fair		Poor
5	4	3	2	1

What went well?

_____

_____

What needs work?

_____

_____

What surprised you?

_____

_____

The next time you do a Kidversation question, what do you want to do differently?

_____

_____

What is the saddest thing that ever happened to you?

Question type: **Emotional**

How can you guide the discussion?
Share your saddest story. Keep it appropriate for the age, but keep it real. Kids find out the truth anyway, and you can build real trust by showing the chinks in your armor. And as your kids hear and see what has happened to you, it helps to validate their own experiences. Seeing that things turned out OK for you helps them to feel the same for themselves.

Parent-to-parent...More insight
Kids suffer. No matter how 'happy' childhood seems, kids often feel sad or slighted or left out. Their wounds are real and can't be glossed over. Empathize with their pain and you take a big step towards helping them heal. Resist the temptation to put their pain or problems into your own 'perspective.' Their feelings are their own - we might not get their problems and pain, but that does not give us the right to deny them. If your kids trust you enough to share what really hurts them, then compassionate listening is the first real step towards a longer-term goal of helping them put their pain into their own life's perspective.

Supporting Questions
- How did you deal with feeling so sad?

- What did you do to feel better?

- What did this experience teach you? How did it make you a better person?

How did the conversation go?

Great		Fair		Poor
5	4	3	2	1

What went well?

_____

_____

What needs work?

_____

_____

What surprised you?

_____

_____

The next time you do a Kidversation question, what do you want to do differently?

_____

_____

What are you most scared of?

Question type: **Emotional**

How can you guide the discussion?
Share your own fears. Be honest and candid. If you are afraid of something happening to your children, share that. If you are scared of things that sound irrational, share that too. Being human is a big step towards being a parent.

Parent-to-parent...More insight
Fear is an incredibly powerful emotion. For younger children, fear is frequently present and is usually pretty easy for them to talk about. For older kids, the fear is still there, but getting it out is harder. Remember to keep an open mind and open heart in case you or something close to you is the cause. But push on gently to get them to share. Help them to understand that most fears can be dealt with (usually with ease) just by naming them and planning a solution. And don't be afraid to suggest going for help outside the family if that is what it takes.

Supporting Questions
- Does this question make you think of personal fears, such as fear of being teased? Or does it make you think of horror movie monsters and other scary things? Or something else? Why?

How did the conversation go?

Great   Fair   Poor

5   4   3   2   1

What went well?

_____

_____

What needs work?

_____

_____

What surprised you?

_____

_____

The next time you do a Kidversation question, what do you want to do differently?

_____

_____

What makes you angry?

Question type: **Emotional**

How can you guide the discussion?

Talk about your own temper. Do you get too angry really quickly? Or are you spaghetti in a windstorm? Admit what your children already know. And if needed, come up with an action plan together to work on your issues and your children's. Starting with "I'm sorry" is usually a big step in dealing with this. After that, help the kids to feel safe reminding you when you lose your temper. They will gain a measure of control and you can work towards a solution.

Parent-to-parent...More insight

Like many things, anger is healthy in moderation. If a kid never gets angry, odds are they are holding back, which is unhealthy. And if they fly into a rage all the time, this is equally unhealthy (and really unpleasant.) Find out what is going on, and help them to understand that moderation is key. It is also really important to understand your own anger issues (and those of other parents/caregivers). Kids usually imitate/react to what they learn in the house. If they see the incredible Hulk at home (MOM ANGRY), they might develop their own anger issues, or they might become spaghetti in a windstorm as a way to feel safer. Look in the mirror first before trying to understand your kids.

Supporting Questions
- Do you get mad 'differently' with different people? For example, is it different getting mad at your friends versus your family?

- When you get angry, how do you calm yourself down? Is this something you can do better?

How did the conversation go?

Great		Fair		Poor
5	4	3	2	1

What went well?

_____

_____

What needs work?

_____

_____

What surprised you?

_____

_____

The next time you do a Kidversation question, what do you want to do differently?

_____

_____

What is your happiest moment?

Question type: **Emotional**

How can you guide the discussion?

What is your happiest memory? Share the things that brought you the greatest joy. And if, like many parents, your happiest moment was the birth of your child, all the better to share. If you can, share moments that include your children and share moments from before you had children. Help them to understand the fullness of your life.

Parent-to-parent...More insight

Finding life's happiest moments with your child is a fantastic gift. If you are part of these memories, all the better. If you are not, don't worry. Plan to make new memories. Focus on the themes that emerge. If all the memories follow a pattern (e.g., vacation, holidays), find ways to explore other happy memories that are outside the pattern. A fun project might be to work with your kids to create a small scrapbook or web page highlighting these memories. Find pictures. Write it down. Use this as an opportunity to do a project together that highlights the good times.

Supporting Questions
- What three things make you happiest?

- Do you feel like happiness comes from outside of you (such as from your friends or from things you own) or does it come from inside of you? Explain.

How did the conversation go?

Great		Fair		Poor
5	4	3	2	1

What went well?

_____

_____

What needs work?

_____

_____

What surprised you?

_____

_____

The next time you do a Kidversation question, what do you want to do differently?

_____

_____

Enjoyment

What is the silliest/funniest thing you've ever done?

Question type: **Enjoyment**

How can you guide the discussion?
When you list your funniest or silliest times, keep in mind you are modeling for your child (no matter their age.) Make sure to include at least one time with the child if at all possible. And remember, humor can often be linked to hard or sad times, so don't be surprised if the conversation turns.

Parent-to-parent...More insight
The secret to this question is not just what you hear, but also what you don't hear. Pay attention to the "who" and "what." Is your child talking about times with friends? With family? The ability to have uncontrolled silly moments is crucial for healthy development. If none of them involve you, think for a moment about how that makes you feel (but keep these thoughts to yourself for now so you do not make them feel badly.) If you want to be part of these moments, ask your kids "What can I do to be more of part of these memories?" and then really listen to the answer.

Supporting Questions
- Who were you with when you did this? Did they think it was as silly or funny as you did?

- What are some other silly or funny times you can share? How about a time when we were funny together?

How did the conversation go?

Great		Fair		Poor
5	4	3	2	1

What went well?

_____

_____

What needs work?

_____

_____

What surprised you?

_____

_____

The next time you do a Kidversation question, what do you want to do differently?

_____

_____

What is your favorite sport to watch?

Question type: **Enjoyment**

> **How can you guide the discussion?**
> If you are into sports, share the story of a big game that happened before your children were born. Use sports as a way to connect to the past. If you are not into sports, talk about why not, but show the effort you are making to bond over whatever they are into. Perhaps this is an opportunity to find a new shared interest.

Parent-to-parent...More insight

Football, baseball, hockey, gymnastics, soccer, the list goes on and on. For so many families, watching a game on TV is a great way to come together. Use these times to bond with your kids on other things outside sports. Use the sport as a gateway to other topics it might be harder to discuss otherwise. Especially for some dads, this might be the most comfortable environment for bringing up the hard topics. But no matter what, keep it fun. If you go too far the other way, they will just find another TV to watch the game.

Supporting Questions
- What is the best game you can remember?

- What is the single biggest or most exciting play?

- What do you think it would be like to play professionally?

How did the conversation go?

	Great		Fair		Poor
	5	4	3	2	1

What went well?

_____

_____

What needs work?

_____

_____

What surprised you?

_____

_____

The next time you do a Kidversation question, what do you want to do differently?

_____

_____

What is your favorite sport to play competitively? For fun?

Question type: **Enjoyment**

How can you guide the discussion?
What did you like to play? Do you have particular memories of either a great moment or a painful moment when playing sports? Use these moments to share with them the life lessons you learned from participating in sports. See if you can tie your own experiences in with your kids. And if you are not into sports, find ways to engage in those your kids care about.

Parent-to-parent...More insight
Sitting on the sidelines watching soccer, football, track, or one of the countless other sporting events your kids might be into is a rite of passage for parents. If you are a serious booster, make sure you do not take it too far. Taking the Parenting Path and teaching your kids balance starts with looking in the mirror at your own choices. And if you've not been around for their games, start the mending process with talk. Ask about a big game, or talk about his or her feelings towards winning and losing - just make sure to meet them where they are, not where you want them to be.

Supporting Questions
- What are some ways you think playing has been good for you?

- Are there any sports you do not play, but wish you did?

How did the conversation go?

Great		Fair		Poor
5	4	3	2	1

What went well?

_____

_____

What needs work?

_____

_____

What surprised you?

_____

_____

The next time you do a Kidversation question, what do you want to do differently?

_____

_____

What hobby or pastime would you like to take up or to do more often?

Question type: **Enjoyment**

> **How can you guide the discussion?**
> Share the hobbies you did when you were younger. Or share some hobbies you've always wanted to do but have not yet started. We all have something we'd learn to do if only we had the time/money/skills. Share yours, and see if it is perhaps something you can start to do with your kids. But if you do, make sure to let them lead. As parents, we have a way of taking over.

Parent-to-parent...More insight
Some parents remember the days of playing marbles, others remember their first video games. Kids today live in a far more complex world, with video games, the Internet, Yu-Gi-Oh and on and on. Arguably, with kids as busy as possible these days, and with so much competing for their attention, a hobby like wood carving or knitting might seem almost quaint (though occasionally trendy so maybe there is hope). See if you can find some common ground, perhaps a hobby you could take up together.

Supporting Questions
- Are there hobbies you wish we could do together?

- What are some ways I can support you in this?

- What are some reasons you think it is important to have a hobby or pastime?

How did the conversation go?

Great		Fair		Poor
5	4	3	2	1

What went well?

_____

_____

What needs work?

_____

_____

What surprised you?

_____

_____

The next time you do a Kidversation question, what do you want to do differently?

_____

_____

Who is your favorite band/musician?

Question type: **Enjoyment**

How can you guide the discussion?
Dust off those old CDs or LPs. Talk with your children about why you still listen to the same Beatles, Nirvana or Luther Vandross albums. Share your passion and see if you can find a link between what they like and what you like. And if you've fallen away from listening to music, start again, and make it a journey you share with your children.

Parent-to-parent...More insight
More than any other form of communication, music is universal and eternal. It is a middle ground where people of all ages can meet. Try on their music - see if you can find parts you like and can relate to. And see if you can get them to do the same for your music. For younger kids, having a dance party to their favorite tunes is a great way to have fun together. For teens, what they listen to is so much a part of who they are. Understand your teen's music and you go a long way to understanding your teen.

Supporting Questions
- Have you ever thought about playing in a band? What do you think that would be like?

- Do you think the life of a musician is glamourous or enviable? What would be hard about being a musician?

How did the conversation go?

Great		Fair		Poor
5	4	3	2	1

What went well?

_____

_____

What needs work?

_____

_____

What surprised you?

_____

_____

The next time you do a Kidversation question, what do you want to do differently?

_____

_____

What is your favorite video game?

Question type: **Enjoyment**

> **How can you guide the discussion?**
> Above all else, don't say Pong. Not unless you are truly a
> geek and a gamer and can say it with sufficient irony. Also,
> don't mention Tetris unless you want to face their scorn and
> derision. Just kidding. But honestly, don't try and appear hip
> or 'in the know' unless you really are. Show genuine interest,
> and then stand back and prepare for an education.

Parent-to-parent...More insight
Gaming is another element that defines
the identity of so many kids today. You might
have strong feelings about games, either the level of violence,
or the seeming anti-social nature, or the lack of physical activity.
You need to walk the fine line between sharing your opinions
without being judgmental. Start by earning some credibility and
trust (go to ign.com and start reading), then help them learn
to be smarter consumers of video games. And if your kids are
younger, keep it safe. They don't need to blow up flesh eating
zombies just yet.

Supporting Questions
- Are there any games coming up that you are really interested in? Tell me about it.

- Are there any old-school/retro games you like?

- Do you play any games that you think I would like? Tell me why.

How did the conversation go?

Great		Fair		Poor
5	4	3	2	1

What went well?

_____

_____

What needs work?

_____

_____

What surprised you?

_____

_____

The next time you do a Kidversation question, what do you want to do differently?

_____

_____

What is your favorite song?

Question type: **Enjoyment**

How can you guide the discussion?
Remember back to when you were younger - especially a teen. Maybe you and an old boyfriend or girlfriend had 'your song' or maybe you and your friends went crazy over one song or another. Most of us used music as our own personal anthem. Share these stories. And if you can, share the songs that make you think of your children. They might get a kick out of hearing how sentimental you can be.

Parent-to-parent...More insight
This changes for kids depending on the month (or day of the week). More than any other stage, kids use particular songs as life anthems. They can't always express themselves, so they let music do it for them. If some of their favorite songs have themes or language you are uncomfortable with (sex, violence or drugs references), you still need to keep an open mind and an open heart. Engaging your child is the most important step towards truly understanding them. And music is the best place to start. Once you've built more trust around this, you can start raising issues around themes and language.

Supporting Questions
- How frequently does your favorite song change?

- How has your taste in music changed over the years?

- What kind of music do you think you will be listening to 10 years from now?

How did the conversation go?

Great		Fair		Poor
5	4	3	2	1

What went well?

_____

_____

What needs work?

_____

_____

What surprised you?

_____

_____

The next time you do a Kidversation question, what do you want to do differently?

_____

_____

Family

What is your best family memory?

Question type: **Family**

How can you guide the discussion?
What are your best family memories with your children?
What are your best family memories with your own parents?
Sharing both will help your children to understand your own
life experiences. Have fun with this and work with the kids to
see if you can pull up some lost memories of good times long
gone.

Parent-to-parent...More insight
Family is such a crucial part of our sense
of self, our definition of who we are. All
families have problems, some much worse than others. But
all families have good times as well. By helping your children
to think about the good times, you can help them to put your
larger family experience in context. And remind them that there
are many more memories yet to be made. Family history is a
living, breathing thing, so embrace it.

Supporting Questions
- Do you feel like we can do something like that again or was that a one time 'best'?

- What are some other great family memories?

- What can we do to make new 'best' memories?

How did the conversation go?

Great   Fair   Poor

5   4   3   2   1

What went well?

_____

_____

What needs work?

_____

_____

What surprised you?

_____

_____

The next time you do a Kidversation question, what do you want to do differently?

_____

_____

What is your worst family memory?

Question type: **Family**

How can you guide the discussion?

Share your worst memories from your current family life and share the worst from when you were growing up. Age appropriate honesty is crucial here and for two reasons - first, kids deserve the truth. They need to know you are real and they might be surprised that you share the same bad memories. And second, hearing these stories from your youth can give them insight into your development and your growth as a person.

Parent-to-parent...More insight

Pretty much everyone has a couple really awful memories that play over and over in their minds. And often, these memories give insight into current fears and worries. In families that dealt with major problems in the past, the act of starting the conversation is itself a big step forward in the healing process. Make sure you are honest - and compassionate - in your reactions to the kids and in telling your own stories. They deserve the truth and can tell if you are lying.

Supporting Questions
- What made it so bad?

- What could we have done differently to fix things?

- What have we learned as a family to keep something like that from happening again?

How did the conversation go?

	Great		Fair		Poor
	5	4	3	2	1

What went well?

_____

_____

What needs work?

_____

_____

What surprised you?

_____

_____

The next time you do a Kidversation question, what do you want to do differently?

_____

_____

What is your favorite thing about me?

Question type: **Family**

How can you guide the discussion?

What did your parents do that was especially fun or great? Think about your favorite things and then ask yourself if you do these same great things with your kids? If not, can you start? Even if you had what you think of as a lousy childhood, you still had good times. Share with your kids so they can understand some of your past.

Parent-to-parent...More insight

Kids perceive everything. They take it all in - both the good and the bad. In opening up the lines of communication, you need to be able to focus the conversation on the good stuff as well as the bad - though some kids really do seem to want to focus on the bad only. Use this as an opportunity to learn what you do that your kids love, to get them to really start talking about the good times. Maybe you can find common ground to make you and your kids happier!

Supporting Questions
- Is this something I do all the time or something that you wish I did more?

- Can you think of reasons why my responsibilities as a parent don't let me be fun 100% of the time?

How did the conversation go?

Great		Fair		Poor
5	4	3	2	1

What went well?

_____

_____

What needs work?

_____

_____

What surprised you?

_____

_____

The next time you do a Kidversation question, what do you want to do differently?

_____

_____

What is your least favorite thing about me?

Question type: **Family**

How can you guide the discussion?

What do you most strongly remember about problems with your parents? What did your parents specifically do that drove you crazy (give details and examples instead of speaking in generalizations)? Think about these, and then ask yourself if you've repeated any of these patterns with your kids. Unless we really think about solving problems created by the past, we tend to repeat them.

Parent-to-parent...More insight

All families have good times and all families have bad times. You want your children to be able to talk about both equally. Check your ego at the door. You need to hear where they feel you are making mistakes. Be open and engage in an honest discussion around what they think. Remember, many kids are very concrete thinkers, so they can be quite harsh and very literal. Take a deep breath and listen, so you can find solutions together. And if you think they need a shift in perspective or if you think they are way off base, you still need to use a soft touch in explaining your position. The critical thinking it takes to shift one's mental position can be tough at times, so taking it slow can only help. And who knows - maybe you are the one who needs to use critical thinking to shift your mental position.

Supporting Questions
- How can I fix this?
- Can you think of any reasons (good or bad) why you think I do this?
- How can you remind me when I am doing the thing you dislike?

How did the conversation go?

Great		Fair		Poor
5	4	3	2	1

What went well?

_____

_____

What needs work?

_____

_____

What surprised you?

_____

_____

The next time you do a Kidversation question, what do you want to do differently?

_____

_____

What is your favorite thing about your siblings?

Question type: **Family**

How can you guide the discussion?
Did you have brothers/sisters? Share your funniest stories, especially the ones that are humbling. This is a chance for you to model behaviors you want to see in your kids, so focus attention on stories that you think will benefit them to hear. And if your relationship with your siblings has been strained, talk to your kids about why, and then brainstorm ways to improve things.

Parent-to-parent...More insight
Ah, the love/hate between siblings. They can be each other's biggest safety-net one moment, and the next they will seem to utterly destroy one another. But pretty much all brothers and sisters have, or at least had good times together. You want to keep your kids focused on their commonalities. If they are already good friends, then great, have fun talking about some of their funniest stories. But if they struggle like so many siblings do, then try and find some positive memories to build on. Help them to think about their connection to each other. But please don't try and guilt them into becoming best friends. It almost never works and ends up pitting them against each other and you. Get them to focus on the positive parts of their relationship, and then build from there.

Supporting Questions
- What are some of your best memories with your siblings?

- Why do you think it is important to have a good relationship with your siblings?

How did the conversation go?

Great   Fair   Poor

5   4   3   2   1

What went well?

_____

_____

What needs work?

_____

_____

What surprised you?

_____

_____

The next time you do a Kidversation question, what do you want to do differently?

_____

_____

What do your siblings do that make you angry?

Question type: **Family**

How can you guide the discussion?
If you had brothers/sisters, odds are high you had your own problems and issues, especially if there were problems at home that caused stress. Be honest with your kids, and remember that every moment, every story offers a teaching experience. If you can, also talk about how these problems changed as you aged and matured. Has time and distance tought you anything?

Parent-to-parent...More insight
Especially in families where there are other problems, siblings can take it out on each other. If your kids struggle to get along, ask yourself why you think this is. Discuss your thoughts with them, but expect this conversation to be a hard one. Kids tend to have incredibly strong emotions towards brothers and sisters - in part because they are forced together, and also because they can be in competition for time, attention and other family resources. Get them to start talking so they can work on healing any rifts. Remember, kids react to the environment created by the parents, so the goal should be to learn how you can rebuild their trust in you and each other.

Supporting Questions
- What do you do that makes them angry with you?

- Can you think of a few things you can do to get along with them better/more often?

- What does fighting with your siblings teach you about life?

How did the conversation go?

Great		Fair		Poor
5	4	3	2	1

What went well?

_____

_____

What needs work?

_____

_____

What surprised you?

_____

_____

The next time you do a Kidversation question, what do you want to do differently?

_____

_____

What is the worst family fight you can remember?

Question type: **Family**

How can you guide the discussion?
First, think back to your childhood. Are there fights/arguments that really stand out? Share with your kids and help them to see what you learned (good or bad). And second, share what you remember about a particular argument or fight that really stands out with your kids. Talk about how it made you feel - scared, angry, frustrated. Odds are high your kids had the same feeling. You can really help to normalize feelings by offering insight into your own emotions.

Parent-to-parent...More insight
Families have fights. Occasional fights are natural. You probably feel like boiling over many more times than you actually do. But for some families, constant fighting is the norm, not the exception. This usually indicates a break down in communication. Maybe you or the kids feel angry and let down. Maybe there are outside tensions that find their way into the home. Kids (and especially teens) can often seem to be the cause of so many arguments. Challenge yourself to think about how you can prevent these arguments. See what you can do to make it easier for them to vent and shout and generally be their explosive selves without you getting pulled into the fray. Remember, listen with an open heart and open mind, turn off your parent-filter and keep them talking.

Supporting Questions
- Do you remember how you felt at the time?

- Looking back, what could we have done to prevent the fight from happening?

- Has anything else like that happened since?

How did the conversation go?

Great   Fair   Poor

5   4   3   2   1

What went well?

_____

_____

What needs work?

_____

_____

What surprised you?

_____

_____

The next time you do a Kidversation question, what do you want to do differently?

_____

_____

What is your favorite part about your bedroom?

Question type: **Family**

How can you guide the discussion?

If you are like many adults, you tend not to think about your room the same way as your kids. You probably don't have posters around, or stuff painted on the walls. Talk to your kids about this shift in priorities, and share what you remember of your childhood room. Make connections between your childhood and theirs.

Parent-to-parent...More insight

Kids use their space to define themselves.

Their bedroom is one of the few places that they can truly call their own. So getting them to talk about their domain is a great way to get them to open up about themselves. And remember, don't critique them or their answers, just listen, process, and share your own experiences. If they can't find anything they like about their room, go the the question on decorating their room as a way to get started.

Supporting Questions
- Why is that your favorite?

- What other parts of your bedroom do you like?

- How has your view of your bedroom changed as you've gotten older?

How did the conversation go?

Great   Fair   Poor

5   4   3   2   1

What went well?

_____

_____

What needs work?

_____

_____

What surprised you?

_____

_____

The next time you do a Kidversation question, what do you want to do differently?

_____

_____

If you could have your bedroom decorated any way, what would you want?

Question type: **Family**

How can you guide the discussion?
Go ahead - admit what you would really do with your bedroom if you could. Want a waterbed - share it! Want a wall full of family photos or perhaps a tiki lounge - talk about it. Most parents are too busy to really think about their own space. Use this as a chance to get your children involved in thinking how your own space can be improved.

Parent-to-parent...More insight
A bedroom can be a blank slate for kids. They see their room as their domain, the only space they really own. So when they talk about how the room could be, they are really talking about ways they envision themselves. Listen for cues and clues, and don't edit or censor them, just listen and engage. And if you can, give them a budget (make it realistic and affordable and stick to it) and let them actually redesign their room, do the shopping, the whole thing - with the stipulation that you are the assistant (and that you have at least some veto power). It will give them a fantastic experience and it will give you a chance to work together.

Supporting Questions

- How would this be different if you could spend as much money as you wanted?

- Can you think of any changes we can make now without spending any money?

- Where should we get started?

How did the conversation go?

	Great		Fair		Poor
	5	4	3	2	1

What went well?

_____

_____

What needs work?

_____

_____

What surprised you?

_____

_____

The next time you do a Kidversation question, what do you want to do differently?

_____

_____

If you could change any one thing about our house/apartment, what would it be?

Question type: **Family**

How can you guide the discussion?
What would you change? There has to be one or more things nagging at you. Use this as an opportunity to work together. Come up with wild and crazy solutions and also see if you can come up with one or more solutions you can actually do together. Then pick one and get started.

Parent-to-parent...More insight
Kids are really perceptive. They notice things we are often too busy to see. So getting their perspective on the house invites them to share their ideas. If they come up with workable ideas on how to change part of your space, go for it! Let them take ownership and see where it takes you. Make it a partnership and set them up for success. Let them take the lead - you get work done and they get a good lesson in managing a project.

Supporting Questions
- Why do you want to make that change?

- If money were no an issue, what other changes would you want to make?

- Can you think of any changes we can make within our budget?

How did the conversation go?

Great   Fair   Poor

5   4   3   2   1

What went well?

_____

_____

What needs work?

_____

_____

What surprised you?

_____

_____

The next time you do a Kidversation question, what do you want to do differently?

_____

_____

What is your strongest memory from a family vacation? Best memory? Worst?

Question type: **Family**

How can you guide the discussion?
Vacations are filled with joy and fraught with peril for many families. Be honest about your own best and worst memories. Talk about vacations from before kids and after kids and about vacations from your own childhood. As they hear about your memories, it will most likely spark their own. It can be fun walking together down memory lane. And if/when bad memories come, be open to discussing them.

Parent-to-parent...More insight
Loading the family into the car, heading out for a vacation into the great unknown. This is one of the few parts of family life that cause us to feel overjoyed while at the same time overwhelmed and perhaps a bit terrified. Expectations are high, problems always arise, and it is all over much too quickly (or not soon enough.) Help your children to remember the good and also see what you can learn from anything that went wrong. The first step in not repeating the mistakes of the past is bringing them out into the sunshine.

Supporting Questions
- Why do you think those memories stand out?

- What are some other strong vacation memories?

- Is that any one vacation we took that you wish we could take again?

How did the conversation go?

Great		Fair		Poor
5	4	3	2	1

What went well?

_____

_____

What needs work?

_____

_____

What surprised you?

_____

_____

The next time you do a Kidversation question, what do you want to do differently?

_____

_____

If you could go anywhere on a family vacation, where would it be?

Question type: **Family**

> **How can you guide the discussion?**
> Be honest. Is your dream vacation a week alone on a beach somewhere. Share that with the kids and explain why (without actually making them feel bad.) Want to take the family to Disney but can't afford it - talk about it and see if you can work with the kids to start saving (an untouchable change jar is a great way to start.)

Parent-to-parent...More insight

Check reality at the door. The kids might not think about the reasons why a vacation on the moon or a month in the Caribbean are equally out of reach, but who cares. Let the kids have fun dreaming and idealizing - heck, join in with them and share the fantasy. And then when you are all done with the impossible, bring it back to the real. What is possible for your family? Find a vacation that works for you and the kids, and then start planning it all out, giving the kids as much responsibility as possible. Have them keep track of the savings. Let them do the research. Let them plan the activities. Let them do as much as is realistic, but be sure to be honest (if something is not affordable, help them to find an alternative you can afford) and keep it fun!

Supporting Questions
- What are some other places you want to visit?

- Can you think of a couple ways we can save to go on the vacation you really want?

How did the conversation go?

Great		Fair		Poor
5	4	3	2	1

What went well?

_____

_____

What needs work?

_____

_____

What surprised you?

_____

_____

The next time you do a Kidversation question, what do you want to do differently?

_____

_____

Friends

Share something about you and your best friend(s) that you've never told me before.

Question type: **Friends**

> **How can you guide the discussion?**
> Share stories of your own experiences with your friends growing up. Tell your kids the stories that helped to define you. They will have fun hearing your stories and will benefit from your experiences. And remember, the goal is to have fun while teaching, so keep the story appropriate while also being honest.

Parent-to-parent...More insight
There is so much complexity in a child's relationship with friends (regardless of age). They can lift each other up and tear each other down. Friends can take the place of family in so many ways - as a source of support, as an identity mirror, as a way to test limits. If you do not understand your kids' friends, you do not understand your kids. And if you have problems with their friends, see if you can find a middle ground. If not, breaking up kids and their friends can be tough, but being separated from your kids because of friends is even harder. Sometimes, you need to find a solution that minimizes problems rather than fully solving them.

Supporting Questions
- What are your favorite things to do with your friends? Is this different for different friends?

- How did you become best friends?

- What do you think your friendship will be like in 5 years?

How did the conversation go?

Great		Fair		Poor
5	4	3	2	1

What went well?

_____

_____

What needs work?

_____

_____

What surprised you?

_____

_____

The next time you do a Kidversation question, what do you want to do differently?

_____

_____

What is the worst fight you've ever had with your best friend(s)?

Question type: **Friends**

> **How can you guide the discussion?**
> As we age, we tend to fight less with our friends. We move to a place where we see them less, and our maturity keeps us from taking disagreements too far. Think back to when you were a kid - describe what you were feeling and thinking then, and how you think about those fights with your friends now. By sharing, you can help to create a road map for your kids to navigate this rough terrain.

Parent-to-parent...More insight
Friends fight. It is a fact of life. Odds are good that your kids have had multiple fights with friends, most of which passed quickly. For some, the fights might seem to overwhelm everything else. Do your best to just listen - don't criticize or judge & no parent filter! If you want to gain deeper insight into your kids, it is crucial that you learn how they cope with peer problems. And if they seem to have toxic friends, kids who just seem to never get along, get your kids to start thinking about whether or not the friendship is worth all the problems. See if you can work together to brainstorm ways to improve these relationships.

Supporting Questions
- What caused the fight?

- How did you make up? Who made the first move?

- Do you ever worry about losing your best friend? Why? How?

How did the conversation go?

Great		Fair		Poor
5	4	3	2	1

What went well?

_____

_____

What needs work?

_____

_____

What surprised you?

_____

_____

The next time you do a Kidversation question, what do you want to do differently?

_____

_____

What is the funniest thing you've ever done with your friends?

Question type: **Friends**

How can you guide the discussion?
First, think about some of your funniest memories from when you were a kid. Odds are, your adult self might not find it all so funny, but tell it anyway (keeping the stories approriate, obviously) to give them insight into your childhood self. Next answer for your adult life. Any similarities? Your kids might enjoy seeing you remember, or they might call you a dork. Regardless, have fun with it and they will most likely come along for the ride!

Parent-to-parent...More insight
If there is one thing you can count on, kids know how to have fun with their friends. They can be any combination of silly, obnoxious, funny, goofy, dramatic, and sometimes even mean. And wow do they think they are funny! Get them talking about something extra funny or goofy, and then stand back because you are bound to hear more than you bargained for. And if ever there is a place to balance turning off your parent-filter with the desire to offer healthy guidance, this is it. If they talk about having done something mean, listen and offer an internalized response such as, "I would probably have felt pretty bad if someone did that to me." The kids feel less like you are judging and more like you are just being a parent, but the lesson will likely stick with them.

Supporting Questions
- Have you ever gotten into trouble for laughing too much with your friends (such as in school)?

- Tell me some other funny things you've done with your friends.

How did the conversation go?

Great		Fair		Poor
5	4	3	2	1

What went well?

_____

_____

What needs work?

_____

_____

What surprised you?

_____

_____

The next time you do a Kidversation question, what do you want to do differently?

_____

_____

Growing Up

What does it mean to be rich?

Question type: **Growing Up**

How can you guide the discussion?
Admit your own money fantasies from when you were a child as well as from your adult life. It is tantalizing to think about how the right amount of cash would make everything better. Talk about the cars you'd drive, the things you'd buy. Just keep in mind the real life lesson you want to teach - money does not, in fact, buy happiness. It just trades problems for problems. How and why people earn money is more important then how much.

Parent-to-parent...More insight
Depending on the age, you could get some funny answers to this one. As you listen to your kids likely talk about what rich people buy, the cars they drive, that sort of thing, you can get a sense of their priorities. Help them to understand the limits of wealth, and the fact that money does not equal happiness. Let them have fun on their little money fantasy, but also keep them grounded in the reality that money seldom leads to joy. And for a good additional dose of parenting, see if you can pull out of them what kind of career they might want that can get them all the wealth they describe, and do some goal setting to get them there.

Supporting Questions
- Do you think people with a lot of money are happier than people without a lot of money? Why?

- Are there hard parts to being rich? What are they?

- Is it more important to work towards being rich or to work towards being happy? Why?

How did the conversation go?

Great		Fair		Poor
5	4	3	2	1

What went well?

_____

_____

What needs work?

_____

_____

What surprised you?

_____

_____

The next time you do a Kidversation question, what do you want to do differently?

_____

_____

Do you want to be famous? If so, how?

Question type: **Growing Up**

How can you guide the discussion?
Did you dream of being famous when you were younger - or do you still? Share it. You are definitely exposing a part of yourself by doing so, especially if you feel you had to give it up, but remember, all kids dream of something big. You were a kid, so talking about and even embracing your past dreams is a great way of modeling how the majority of people who do not 'make it' are happy. And if you are not at peace with your life, work with your kids to find ways to make it so.

Parent-to-parent...More insight
An actor? A world famous singer? A best selling author? There are so many ways kids idealize being famous. They see stars and other famous people on magazine covers and on the screen and they think, "That could be me." Listen to what they say, and remember that especially for kids, dreams are fragile and dangerously sharp and jagged when broken. Don't criticize or edit, just listen with an open mind and open heart. And never, ever tell them all the reasons they can't reach their dream - even if you believe it to be true. Rather, help them to do the research and get them thinking about all the work it takes to get 'there' in the first place. If they are willing to do the work, great! They will remember your support and love, just as they will remember your discouragement, regardless of whether or not they ever 'make it big.' The most sincere form of failure is the failure to try.

Supporting Questions
- What do you think are the downsides to being famous?

- How would your life change if people knew you and wanted to talk to you everywhere you went?

How did the conversation go?

Great		Fair		Poor
5	4	3	2	1

What went well?

_____

_____

What needs work?

_____

_____

What surprised you?

_____

_____

The next time you do a Kidversation question, what do you want to do differently?

_____

_____

Do you ever dream of being able to do something that might feel impossible or out of reach?

Question type: **Growing Up**

How can you guide the discussion?
Did you want to walk on the moon or dive to the bottom of an ocean trench? Share. And thinking about dreams you have now as an adult (another question deals with lost dreams from childhood), what would you do if your time, energy, effort, cost, etc. were not barriers? Be brave enough to share with your kids, and maybe you can find a way to work together to make your dreams a reality.

Parent-to-parent...More insight
We all have dreams. As younger kids, the idea of traveling in space or becoming president is no less realistic than pizza maker or teacher. As we get older, life's practical side steps in and we hone down or even cut off these dreams. This is a tragedy we can prevent. Dreaming makes us better than we are today - so long as we work towards them. Help your kids to understand that reaching their dreams is hard work. Most people who sit around waiting for luck almost never realize their dreams. And odds are high your kids will share a lightning-strikes story, "She was discovered singing karaoke." Help them to see that waiting for lightning to strike is not the best long-term strategy.

Supporting Questions
- Why is it important to have dreams? How do dreams make us better people?

- What can you do to work towards accomplishing your dreams?

How did the conversation go?

Great		Fair		Poor
5	4	3	2	1

What went well?

_____

_____

What needs work?

_____

_____

What surprised you?

_____

_____

The next time you do a Kidversation question, what do you want to do differently?

_____

_____

Have you ever given up on any of your dreams?

Question type: **Growing Up**

How can you guide the discussion?
Self-truth time. Walking away from your dreams can be really tough for some. Life can really get in the way, or so it feels. What did you walk away from (regrets or not?) Is there any way to involve your kids in working towards your dreams again? Part of growing up and finding true happiness is making peace with the people we become. If you've not done so, start talking with your kids about how you can.

Parent-to-parent...More insight
You might struggle to ask your kids this for a few reasons. First, they are kids, so how can they have already given up? And second, you might feel raw about your own lost dreams. Either way, swallow your assumptions (and pride) and listen. Kids dream and they dream really big (and sometimes really small.) Their "internal life" is crucial for their healthy development. So just listen, keeping an open mind and open heart. Resist the urge to save them, and please don't discount or invalidate what they are saying. For them, it is as real as can be. Your compassion and ability to listen will connect you to them.

Supporting Questions
- What is the difference between giving up on your dreams and having your dreams change as you age?

- If your dream is important enough, what can you do to work towards making it happen?

How did the conversation go?

Great		Fair		Poor
5	4	3	2	1

What went well?

_____

_____

What needs work?

_____

_____

What surprised you?

_____

_____

The next time you do a Kidversation question, what do you want to do differently?

_____

_____

If you/we could move anywhere in the world, where would it be?

Question type: **Growing Up**

How can you guide the discussion?
Where would you like to move? Is there anyplace you've dreamed of going? Maybe you lived someplace before having kids. Share the details. Fill in the gaps so they can see you as someone who came from somewhere and thinks about new places to go and explore.

Parent-to-parent...More insight
This can tell you a few things. Kids can seem to have a fairly limited view of the world. This question will give you a sense of how broad their perspective really is. Listen closely, and then have fun with wherever they say they want to go. Do some research together about their desired area – check out housing costs and the job market. A little family fantasy can be fun. Who knows where it will lead you? Why not move to Hawaii!?

Supporting Questions
- Is there anyplace you would never want to live? Why?

- Why do you think we chose to live where we do?

- Can you think of life choices you can make that will someday allow you to live where you want?

How did the conversation go?

Great   Fair   Poor

5   4   3   2   1

What went well?

_____

_____

What needs work?

_____

_____

What surprised you?

_____

_____

The next time you do a Kidversation question, what do you want to do differently?

_____

_____

What work do you want to do when you grow up?

Question type: **Growing Up**

How can you guide the discussion?
Are you doing the work you really want to do? If you are like many adults, you are thinking that you don't know what you want to be when you grow up either. That is fine. In fact, working on that and involving the kids is a great way to build strong connections. This can be a fantastic opportunity for you to explore for yourself. And remember, you are never too old to make a change!

Parent-to-parent...More insight
Depending on the age, you will see a lot of variety in this. At younger ages, kids have a vague sense of work. Help them to think about how people are needed to make all parts of society function. As the kids get older and work starts to become a reality, start them thinking about ways to translate interests into careers. And work together to explore various options. This is a great opportunity to help kids to make the connection between having dreams and actually working towards them. If they want to be scientists, look for clubs at school or competitions. If they want to be something you know little about, do research together and take them to visit professionals in the field. It will be fun and can really connect them to their ideas.

Supporting Questions
- What type of preparation do you think you will have to do for that kind of work?

- Tell me some of the reasons why that is what you want to do for work?

- Tell me about other work you might want to do.

How did the conversation go?

Great		Fair		Poor
5	4	3	2	1

What went well?

_____

_____

What needs work?

_____

_____

What surprised you?

_____

_____

The next time you do a Kidversation question, what do you want to do differently?

_____

_____

Personal

What is your favorite color? What do people's favorite colors say about them?

Question type: **Personal**

How can you guide the discussion?
Perhaps it has been a while since you've thought about your favorite color - maybe not. For kids young and old, color is one of the very visible ways they can show the world how they see themselves. So what 'color' are you? And make sure to check out the details below on what the colors we like say about us.

Parent-to-parent...More insight
Many people believe color preference can give you insight into a person. Whether or not you agree, society tends to divide gender based on color preference. Here is a really quick primer on what color theory says about a person. Take it with a grain of salt and do more research if you or the kids are really interested. White: Simplicity, purity, innocence and naïveté. Red: The color of strength, health, vitality, possibly aggression. Pink: Gentle, loving, nurturing. Orange: Luxurious, pleasure-seeking, flamboyant and fun-loving person. Often restless. Yellow: Happiness, wisdom and imagination. Might not accept responsibility. Green: Harmony and balance, hope, renewal and peace. Potentially easy to manipulate. Blue: Soft, soothing, compassionate and caring, deliberate and thoughtful. Can be detached and can refuse help. Black: Authoritative and powerful. Purple: Highly individual, witty sensitive, strong desire to be unique. Often temperamental.

Supporting Questions
- Are there any ways that you try and bring your favorite color into your life more (your room, clothes, etc.)?

- Can you ever have TOO much of this color?

- What are your least favorite colors?

How did the conversation go?

Great   Fair   Poor

5   4   3   2   1

What went well?

_____

_____

What needs work?

_____

_____

What surprised you?

_____

_____

The next time you do a Kidversation question, what do you want to do differently?

_____

_____

What is your favorite animal? What animal do you feel most reflects who you are?

Question type: **Personal**

How can you guide the discussion?
What was your favorite animal as a child? What animals did you see in the zoo or circus that really impressed or scared you? Do you have a favorite animal now? Have fun with this question. As a teen, how did this change for you? Were there pets or other animals that you related to during your years of teen angst?

Parent-to-parent...More insight
For younger children, animals play a big role in learning and development (think of many children's books). As they age, most kids still maintain a love of animals. And finally for tweens and teens, animals are often a way to start thinking about the natural world around us. It turns out that sharks are not just cool, but they also tell us a lot about the world we live in! Use this as an opportunity to explore an animal of interest to you and your kids. One quick example - research the ways frogs are one of the best indicators of environmental problems. A bit of digging (try local environmental organizations) and you can find out which animals in your area help to measure your environment's health. Use this as an excuse to get the kids out on a hike.

Supporting Questions
- If you could have your very own pet, what would it be?

- Tell my about some animals in the world that are in danger of extinction? Why is it important to not let animals become extinct?

How did the conversation go?

Great		Fair		Poor
5	4	3	2	1

What went well?

_____

_____

What needs work?

_____

_____

What surprised you?

_____

_____

The next time you do a Kidversation question, what do you want to do differently?

_____

_____

What is your favorite site on the Internet?

Question type: Personal

How can you guide the discussion?
What sites do you like? What do you use for work versus interest or recreation? Talk about how the Internet has changed things so dramatically. Most kids these days only know a world with the Internet. Talk about some of the things you used to do in the real world that now happens largely on the Internet. It will give them a good chance to laugh at you.

Parent-to-parent...More insight
The Internet can be a daunting place to send your children. We want to protect them and keep them away from the bad elements. But there is lots of good information and fun to be had. Engage them fully in their Internet usage. Learn where they go and what they do so you can help to protect them, while at the same time understanding a More about their world. But don't be daunted or give up if they try and keep you away. One quick suggestion - find sites they go to most frequently, then go there yourself. Explore their world a bit. Ignorance poses the single greatest risk.

Supporting Questions
- Do you worry about issues like privacy or security when you go on the Internet? Why?

- What are the different ways you use computers and the Internet in school?

How did the conversation go?

Great		Fair		Poor
5	4	3	2	1

What went well?

_____

_____

What needs work?

_____

_____

What surprised you?

_____

_____

The next time you do a Kidversation question, what do you want to do differently?

_____

_____

What is your favorite dessert?

Question type: **Personal**

How can you guide the discussion?
Is it a chocolate chip cookie dipped in milk? Or perhaps Flan? Do any really strange desserts stand out to you (chocolate covered jalapeños perhaps?) Is there a treat you remember from childhood that you have not had in a long time? Think back and share memories of a particularly big or interesting dessert.

Parent-to-parent...More insight
Everyone loves dessert, so have fun!
Explore interesting desserts you can make together. Try Kheer rice pudding from India or Moon Cakes from China. Explore desserts you've never had before. Then settle in for some chocolate chip cookies and plan future adventures in sweets. Talk about a comfort dessert from your childhood, and see if you can find the recipe to make together. But don't be surprised if it tastes little like your memory!

Supporting Questions
- Is there any dessert that you've always wanted to try but have never had?

- Can you remember any dessert you did not like?

- What are your three favorite types of cookies?

How did the conversation go?

Great		Fair		Poor
5	4	3	2	1

What went well?

_____

_____

What needs work?

_____

_____

What surprised you?

_____

_____

The next time you do a Kidversation question, what do you want to do differently?

_____

_____

What is your favorite restaurant?

Question type: **Personal**

How can you guide the discussion?

How have your tastes changed since you were a kid? What are your strongest memories of going to restaurants with your parents? Was there one dish in particular you always wanted? What did it taste like and how did it make you feel to order it? Going out can be defining family experiences (for good or bad), so share how these experiences made you feel. And if you had one of those families that never went out to eat, talk about why that was and how that made you feel.

Parent-to-parent...More insight

It can be really tough for kids and parents to agree on a restaurant. Younger ones would go to a certain pizza/arcade named after a big mouse all the time. Some kids (and maybe parents) want nothing but the place with the clown. But restaurants are a way to explore many cultures and perspectives. If you and/or your kids are hesitant to try new places, work together to come up with a list of restaurants and types of cuisine to try. Then talk about what everyone liked and disliked. As our world keeps getting smaller and our country is increasingly multicultural, food is a great place to start exploring new cultures.

Supporting Questions
- What is the most expensive or luxurious meal you can remember eating?

- Is there a restaurant you've always wanted to try?

- How does eating food from other countries help us to better understand other people/cultures?

How did the conversation go?

Great		Fair		Poor
5	4	3	2	1

What went well?

_____

_____

What needs work?

_____

_____

What surprised you?

_____

_____

The next time you do a Kidversation question, what do you want to do differently?

_____

_____

What is your best holiday memory? Worst?

Question type: **Personal**

How can you guide the discussion?
What are your strongest memories from your own childhood celebrations? Think back to the good and the bad. Share these memories along with your feelings then, and now looking back. Help your kids to understand how time and distance can change your perspective.

Parent-to-parent...More insight
Holidays were made for kids and families. Regardless of tradition, holidays are a time of celebration and fun. They can also be a time when emotions run high and kids can have really high expectations. And for some families, they are a time when family problems can become focused and magnified. Get your kids to talk about their best memories, and then have them talk about some of the bad ones. Help them to accept and embrace what went right in addition to what went wrong. And if the holidays have been been a time of frustration or pain for your family, talk openly about what you can do differently in the future.

Supporting Questions
- Why do you think the holidays are so important?

- Tell me about some of your favorite traditions when celebrating this holiday.

- What one food do you most associate with this holiday?

How did the conversation go?

Great		Fair		Poor
5	4	3	2	1

What went well?

_____

_____

What needs work?

_____

_____

What surprised you?

_____

_____

The next time you do a Kidversation question, what do you want to do differently?

_____

_____

If you could design the perfect celebration for your favorite holiday, what would it be?

Question type: **Personal**

How can you guide the discussion?
What would you do differently? Does your family celebrate the holidays the way you want? Or have you settled for the easiest or most extended-family friendly approach? 'Aunt Edna must have dinner at 1 in the afternoon!' Share your own wishes. Then explore whether any of these wishes can be made into reality, or if not, why not? See if the kids can make suggestions.

Parent-to-parent...More insight
This is a great fantasy exercise. As the parent, you need to check your own, more mature sense of reality at the door. Let your kids have a great fantasy version of what the holidays can be. Stacks of presents? Celebrating in Paris? Getting away from mom and dad? Let them explore it all. Then see if there are any threads you can pick up together and make into reality. It would be great if the kids could come up with a new tradition.

Supporting Questions
- Would you want to stay home or travel?
- What kind of food would be served?
- Would you invite friends, or would it just be family, or both?

How did the conversation go?

Great		Fair		Poor
5	4	3	2	1

What went well?

_____

_____

What needs work?

_____

_____

What surprised you?

_____

_____

The next time you do a Kidversation question, what do you want to do differently?

_____

_____

What is your favorite book?

Question type: **Personal**

> **How can you guide the discussion?**
> Think back. Do you remember the magic and power of one book or another from when you were a child? Was there a special book that really impacted you? Do you still read in your adult life? Regardless, work with your kids to find books you can read together.

Parent-to-parent...More insight

Books can be powerful and transformative for kids. More than TV or video games, books can transport kids to another place, let them try on other people's experiences. Unfortunately, many kids see reading as something they are forced to do in school. If your kids already love reading, or if they see it as something less than enjoyable, work to find a book you and they can enjoy together. Connecting over the pages of a book is one of the best ways to build a long-term love of reading.

Supporting Questions
- Why is it your favorite book?

- Tell me about the characters and the plot?

- What are some other books you love?

- What are some books you are looking forward to reading?

How did the conversation go?

Great		Fair		Poor
5	4	3	2	1

What went well?

_____

_____

What needs work?

_____

_____

What surprised you?

_____

_____

The next time you do a Kidversation question, what do you want to do differently?

_____

_____

What is your favorite TV show?

Question type: **Personal**

How can you guide the discussion?

What were your favorite shows as a kid? How do they compare to the shows your kids watch today? How has your taste changed over time? If you feel you or your kids watch too much TV, work on a plan to cut down by talking about entertainment and relaxation alternatives. Go back to the question on reading for some ideas!

Parent-to-parent...More insight

Just like adults, kids use TV for entertainment and to escape the pressures of everyday life. The question you need to ask is if you are supporting healthy TV watching in your kids (and yourself)? How much TV is enough? Too much inactivity (like couch surfing) leads to obesity, illness, and for many kids, isolation from others their age. Work with them to understand that TV, in moderation, can be great. But too much TV is like any other drug - bad news. And think about the type of TV they are watching. Is it appropriate for their age? Does it reflect the values you want to instill in your kids? As the parent, you are responsible for what they watch. And helping them to make good TV choices will benefit them at home, in school, and throughout their lives.

Supporting Questions
- Why is it your favorite show?
- Do you think TV is healthy for kids (and adults)?
- How much is too much?

How did the conversation go?

Great		Fair		Poor
5	4	3	2	1

What went well?

_____

_____

What needs work?

_____

_____

What surprised you?

_____

_____

The next time you do a Kidversation question, what do you want to do differently?

_____

_____

Who is your favorite character from a book or comic book?

Question type: **Personal**

How can you guide the discussion?

Do you remember your favorite characters growing up? What in particular did you identify with? Was there a character that troubled you, that you thought about long after? Show your kids how the complexity of the best book characters often helps us to understand our own lives - even as adults.

Parent-to-parent...More insight

Whether its Harry Potter or Batman someone you've never heard of, odds are high your child has really identified with a character, either fictional or from nonfiction. Books are a great way to connect with characters because we experience their lives and adventures so closely. Explore what it is about the character your child identifies with and learn what you can, going so far as to read story yourself. What insights can you gather that can help you to understand your child? And then see if you can find similar books for them to read (the library is a beautiful thing). They will appreciate your active interest.

Supporting Questions
- What is it about the character that makes you like him/her so much?

- Tell me some examples of things he/she has done that you thought were great.

How did the conversation go?

Great	Fair	Poor
5 4	3	2 1

What went well?

_____

_____

What needs work?

_____

_____

What surprised you?

_____

_____

The next time you do a Kidversation question, what do you want to do differently?

_____

_____

Who is your favorite character from a TV show or movie?

Question type: **Personal**

How can you guide the discussion?
What characters do you remember from growing up? Why did you particularly identify with one character over another? Do you remember how you felt when you were most engaged with the show, how you felt when something particularly interesting or bad happened? Share, and then share how you view TV now versus then. Help your kids to understand how our views change over time, as we come to realize that TV shows do not usually reflect reality (and that is especially true for reality tv shows!)

Parent-to-parent...More insight
The days of Saturday morning cartoons are long gone! Now we have whole networks dedicated to cartoons. So is the time when kids had to wait a whole week to see what would happen next to their favorite character. Tivo, DVRs, and Internet video have changed all that. But at the heart of it, the ability of TV to show us characters we love and understand has not changed. When we see characters on screen, and we see them going through different stories every week - solving problems, falling in love, escaping danger - people build close familiariaty with those characters. Help kids to understand that these characters are fiction, not real, and do not reflect reality. Kids might not admit it, but seeing the idealized versions of reality on TV can seriously influence how they think about their own lives.

Supporting Questions
- What about the character is appealing to you?

- Has the character been consistent across shows or movie sequels?

- What is the character's back story? Where did he/she come from?

How did the conversation go?

Great	Fair	Poor

5   4   3   2   1

What went well?

_____

_____

What needs work?

_____

_____

What surprised you?

_____

_____

The next time you do a Kidversation question, what do you want to do differently?

_____

_____

What is your first memory ever?

Question type: **Personal**

How can you guide the discussion?
What is your first memory of your kids? Help them fill in the gaps to when they were born. Help to put the brief span of their lives into the context of your much longer life. This can be an emotional topic, so don't be afraid to show how looking back can make even the most cynical person a bit wistful and sad.

Parent-to-parent...More insight
Another way to ask this question is "What is your strongest early memory?" There tends to be one thing or another that really stands out in memory. The past needs to stay with us, to help us remember where we come from in our lives. As concrete thinkers and with limited perspective, time can be a tough concept for kids. Yesterday can seem like an eternity ago and a year ago can seem like yesterday. So help them to focus on the memories that really have a larger meaning. One thing that can help is a memory journal - writing out recollections, collecting photos, that sort of thing. It is a great opportunity to reflect on the passage of time together, just don't be surprised when you and your kids have vastly different impressions of the speed at which time passes.

Supporting Questions
- Why do you think that one memory stands out?

- Do you remember how you felt at the time?

- What are some other memories from your earliest days?

How did the conversation go?

Great		Fair		Poor
5	4	3	2	1

What went well?

_____

_____

What needs work?

_____

_____

What surprised you?

_____

_____

The next time you do a Kidversation question, what do you want to do differently?

_____

_____

If you could have any one additional freedom/right/privilege, what would it be?

Question type: **Personal**

How can you guide the discussion?

Did you feel especially limited as a child? Do you feel you give your kids too much or too little space? We tend to either repeat parts of our past with our kids, or we go in the opposite direction, to rebel against what we perceive as problems from our own past. Identify these trends, and then work with your kids to find a rational middle path that balances safety and responsibility with age appropriate freedom.

Parent-to-parent...More insight

You can guarantee every kid is going to feel limited and oppressed at one point or another. From the youngest ages through high school and beyond, kids always want more freedom. But as parents, it is our right and responsibility to keep our kids safe and to limit them to things that are appropriate. And we should never permit anything illegal. If you take a reasonable stand as a parent, you can often get your kids to at least listen to your reasons. And if you find you are limiting your kids for irrational reasons ("I'm the parent, that's why!" is not really a rational reason in most kids' eyes), work together to find ways to test out new levels of responsibility. If they earn additional rights and responsibilities, recognizing this is a great step in helping them to mature. This can be started at any age.

Supporting Questions
* What are some ways you can build the trust to earn the additional rights and freedoms?

* Do you feel like you have more or fewer priviledges than your friends? How do they earn or lose these priviledges?

How did the conversation go?

Great   Fair   Poor

5   4   3   2   1

What went well?

_____

_____

What needs work?

_____

_____

What surprised you?

_____

_____

The next time you do a Kidversation question, what do you want to do differently?

_____

_____

Do you have nightmares? What do you remember and why do you think you have them?

Question type: **Personal**

> **How can you guide the discussion?**
> Start the sentence "I remember this one nightmare where…"
> Kids need to hear your nightmares as well. This is an opportunity to show them how normal and even necessary it is for our minds to handle big and difficult problems. Our dreams are one of the ways we cope, so show them how it worked for you.

Parent-to-parent…More insight
Our dreams. This is where we work out the things that we often struggle to deal with in our waking lives. Kids are no different. Nightmare are ways for kids to define and cope with the mass of problems that are swirling around in their heads. For kids to share, they need to feel safe, to feel you will listen compassionately and without judging. And while some nightmares are just plain strange, even the scariest nightmares can be amazing teachers. You need to be ready to learn just as much as your child does. Rather than focusing on saving them from their terrible dreams, focus on steps they can take to address the underlying worries and problems that are bothering them in the first place.

Supporting Questions
- Where do you think nightmares come from?

- What are some ways nightmares can help us? What are they trying to teach us?

- What is the funniest dream you can remember?

How did the conversation go?

Great		Fair		Poor
5	4	3	2	1

What went well?

_____

_____

What needs work?

_____

_____

What surprised you?

_____

_____

The next time you do a Kidversation question, what do you want to do differently?

_____

_____

Do you think you are good looking?

Question type: **Personal**

How can you guide the discussion?

Some of us leave these types of concerns behind us as we age, some of us never leave them behind. But think back to how you felt as a kid. Think of the first time (if ever) you were teased because of your looks. Or the first time you teased someone else. The truth is, kids can be brutal. Offer your own history as a way to connect on a tough issue. And if there is any pain in the past, be honest about it with your kids. It will do all of you good.

Parent-to-parent...More insight

Warning. This is a loaded question for most kids. They want to be seen as good looking. But as they get older, all kids go through awkward stages. And the pressure from others at school makes this even harder. Talk about peer pressure and how there can be very narrow ideas around the concept of 'good looking' in many schools. And listen compassionately, knowing it can be tough. On the flip side, if your child is vain, if they feel they are really good looking, how do you help them balance this with kindness for others? At the same time, they will likely talk about how they feel about the looks of others. Help them to understand that there are MANY different types of beauty (not just what they see on TV or magazines) that go far beyond the surface of the person. Help your kids to develop a healthy attitude towards their own looks and the looks of others by helping them to understand that what we see on the surface is not the whole person.

Supporting Questions
- How does this question make you feel? Embarrassed at all?

- Tell me one attractive or beautiful thing about yourself? Your siblings? Your friends?

How did the conversation go?

Great		Fair		Poor
5	4	3	2	1

What went well?

_____

_____

What needs work?

_____

_____

What surprised you?

_____

_____

The next time you do a Kidversation question, what do you want to do differently?

_____

_____

Do you like yourself?

Question type: **Personal**

How can you guide the discussion?
Do you struggle with self-doubt and uncertainty? Everyone has these moments. How has this changed since you were a kid? Do you feel better or worse about yourself now? Why? As a parent, you need to balance sharing the truth (which kids figure out anyway) with the responsibility of setting a good example. If you have self-worth issues, be candid, but also discuss how you are dealing with it. Ask for ideas about how you can work together on these issues. Odds are, they already know, so let them be part of the solution.

Parent-to-parent...More insight
This is at the core of so many struggles for kids, especially teenagers. Even younger kids go through stages of fear and self-doubt. And as teenagers, all of life's challenges can build up to make them feel like their own worst critic. Struggles with school, friends, parents, sports (the list goes on) can make even the most positive kids have moments of doom and gloom. As a parent, your job is to help your child understand that what happens around them is not the only way to see themselves. Kids need to develop a sense of self-worth that is internally driven (by their own belief that they are good, honest, lovable, etc.) and not by the world around them. You can't protect them from everything, but you can help them develop the attitudes and sense of self-worth to weather most storms.

Supporting Questions
- Tell me your three favorite things about yourself?

- Tell me the difference between liking yourself (even loving yourself) and being vain?

- What do your friends like most about you?

How did the conversation go?

Great		Fair		Poor
5	4	3	2	1

What went well?

_____

_____

What needs work?

_____

_____

What surprised you?

_____

_____

The next time you do a Kidversation question, what do you want to do differently?

_____

_____

Is there anything about yourself you would change if you could?

Question type: **Personal**

How can you guide the discussion?
At one point or another, everyone has made the "if only" wish. "If only I was smarter/better looking, more popular, etc." Talk about what you wished to change about yourself when you were younger. And then explore how these wishes changed as you got older. Part of our life's work as adults is to explore what we do and why. If you are wishing to be someone you are not, this is a good chance to work together to explore who you really are, and what you want to become.

Parent-to-parent...More insight
Pretty much everyone at one point has thought "If I could only change...", thinking they were one change away from happiness. Whether to be better looking, a better athlete, smarter, or any of the other self-doubts kids tend to have, wishing for that one change that makes it all better is pretty typical. Start out having fun with this exercise if possible, but the move towards discussing one of two things – either how to make it happen (e.g. they want to do better in school) or why it is not necessary (e.g. they want to be better looking). When taken together, balancing self-acceptance and a will to change can do wonders. The hard truth is, none of these wishes really translate to happiness. Feeling better comes from inside of us, not from any of the types of changes we wish for as children.

Supporting Questions
- Are these changes on the surface or deeper down?

- What does it take to change different aspects of who you are? What is the work involved?

- How can you learn to make peace and find acceptance with this part of yourself?

How did the conversation go?

Great   Fair   Poor

5   4   3   2   1

What went well?

_____

_____

What needs work?

_____

_____

What surprised you?

_____

_____

The next time you do a Kidversation question, what do you want to do differently?

_____

_____

School

Have you ever been bullied or bullied anyone?

Question type: **School**

How can you guide the discussion?
Were you bullied or did you bully anyone? In the past, people used to pass off bullying as kids being kids, but no more. Was there someone whom you intimidated or who intimidated you? Be honest about this. Your kids will benefit to hear solutions you may have come up with, or at least how it made you feel, why you think it happened. For many adults, this is a topic that can still be emotionally raw. But keeping it buried in the past denies you healing and your kids the chance to see how bullying hurts long after. Honesty is key to get your kids to be honest with you.

Parent-to-parent...More insight
Unfortunately, bullying is very much a reality in many kids lives. And it is not just the really big and obvious kind. Bullying happens in often subtle ways. Maybe it is intimidation. Maybe it is on the Internet, or on email, or through texts on a mobile phone. Maybe it is cruel teasing. But it usually has to do with someone exerting power over someone else. If your child is involved in bullying (either side), get the school counselor involved and work to find out why it is happening. Your anger (again, for either side) and sadness will not help long-term. This is a problem that needs a parental and school solution. And be candid with your kids about why this is serious and what you plan to do about it. Work with them - they will often push hard against making it a bigger problem, typically out of fear. Help them to understand that there are adults who can and will help.

Supporting Questions
- What are the different forms bullying can take?

- Is bullying using social networks (Facebook) and cell phone texting more, less or just as hurtful as bullying in person?

- Tell me some examples of bullying you've seen.

How did the conversation go?

Great		Fair		Poor
5	4	3	2	1

What went well?

_____

_____

What needs work?

_____

_____

What surprised you?

_____

_____

The next time you do a Kidversation question, what do you want to do differently?

_____

_____

What is your favorite thing about school? Least favorite?

Question type: **School**

How can you guide the discussion?

What do you remember about school? Are there any particular memories that really stand out. Share the good and the bad. Give some insight into your own joys and struggles. While it will help the kids to see some adult perspective, it will also give you a chance to empathize and connect with their current circumstances. Time changes how we view our time in school. Help them to see how time has changed your perspective, How has maturing changed the way you view the past?

Parent-to-parent...More insight

For most kids, school ranks as the single biggest part of their day, and sometimes the biggest part of their lives. It can be a great place for some, and a terrible place for others. As adults looking back, we tend to either gloss over the bad stuff we dealt with - "school was the BEST!" Or we tend to overemphasize problems - "school was the WORST!" But your kids are in the middle of it, and school life can be really hard. From popularity to peer pressure, academic pressure and sports pressure, kids spend their days in a pressure cooker. You can help them out just by being a safe and sane listening ear. Start the discussion to help them put it all into perspective so they can be mindful of the good as well as the difficult.

Supporting Questions
- What are some ways your attitude impacts your success and how much you enjoy going to school?

- What has changed over the years about your attitude towards school? How do you think it will change in the future?

How did the conversation go?

Great		Fair		Poor
5	4	3	2	1

What went well?

_____

_____

What needs work?

_____

_____

What surprised you?

_____

_____

The next time you do a Kidversation question, what do you want to do differently?

_____

_____

What scares you most about moving to the next grade? What are you most excited for?

Question type: **School**

How can you guide the discussion?
How do you deal with big transitions now? How did you feel back when you were transitioning between schools? Share one or more defining moments - a new friend; a teacher you connected with; some problem or confrontation. Remember, we are teaching with our examples, so be honest, but share a message that will resonate.

Parent-to-parent...More insight
There is so much transition for kids. Every few years they jump to a new school, facing a new set of expectations. Time might seem to crawl for them, but for parents it thunders by. Each transition brings a new opportunity for change and growth, a new sign of potential for kids. But these are also scary times, when facing the unknown can be intimidating. Talk about how to best face it all, and see what kind of support you can offer, so you can face it together. And help them to understand that the transition every few years is a chance to try new things and to reinvent parts of themselves.

Supporting Questions
- What do you think the single biggest change will be when you have to switch buildings again (such as going from middle school to high school)?

- Do you feel like each new grade presents a new opportunity for you, or do you feel like things don't change much from year to year?

How did the conversation go?

Great		Fair		Poor
5	4	3	2	1

What went well?

_____

_____

What needs work?

_____

_____

What surprised you?

_____

_____

The next time you do a Kidversation question, what do you want to do differently?

_____

_____

Do you want to go to college? If so, where? If not, then what do you want to do?

Question type: **School**

How can you guide the discussion?
Talk about why you did or did not go to college, and what you would do the same or differently now. We can guide kids with words, but our actions also send a strong message. Find out what they are thinking, and how that aligns with your wishes. And if you hear plans that do not kilter with your expectations, getting angry will only create more problems. Instead, calmly frame your concerns in 'I' statements, as in "I would worry about my future if..." If you can share with compassion and love, you will be in a better position and they will be more likely to listen to you.

Parent-to-parent...More insight
The decision to go to college (or not) plays a huge role in most kids high school experience.
As a parent, you need to find a way encourage your child's interests and their ideas (even if you disagree with them) while at the same time keeping in mind the 'long game' that might elude their thinking. There are two painfully conflicting facts here - college is not for everyone, but on average, those who go to college make considerably more money and have more life opportunities than those who do not. It is oddly backwards that teens are expected to make choices that impact the remainder of their lives. So you need to be a trusted and important partner and counselor to your kids to help them make the best long-term decision. By thinking and planning as early as possible and by working together, you can find a way to navigate this potentially difficult terrain.

Supporting Questions
- How do you think your life would be different if you did the opposite of what you want to do (e.g. if you went to college but did not want to, or if you wanted to go to college but did not)?

- If you are not planning to go to college right away after high school, do you think you will ever go?

How did the conversation go?

Great	Fair	Poor
5 4	3 2	1

What went well?

_____

_____

What needs work?

_____

_____

What surprised you?

_____

_____

The next time you do a Kidversation question, what do you want to do differently?

_____

_____

What do you want to study when you go to college?

Question type: **School**

> **How can you guide the discussion?**
> What did you study in college (or what would you have wanted to study if you'd gone)? Do you feel that your major has helped or hindered you in your adult and professional life? What would you do differently now? If you did not go to college but would still like to, include your kids in your thinking and planning. Maybe they will be the motivation you need to make it happen.

Parent-to-parent...More insight

It is a cruel twist of fate that has young adults, with little life experience, make decisions about their major, something that could impact the rest of their lives. Many people often go in different directions than their undergraduate major would suggest. By working with your child, you can be a source of information and support in this decision process. Help them to see this is not a life or death decision, but one that should support a lifetime of learning. The high school counselor is a great place to start - set up a meeting to review your child's current status and then set a game plan. The goal is not to place undue pressure on your child, but to find out where pressure already exists so you can develop a healthy approach for moving forward.

Supporting Questions
- Why do you think that is what you want to study?

- What are some other topics or ideas you would like to explore when you go to college?

- Is there anything about going to college that scares you?

How did the conversation go?

Great		Fair		Poor
5	4	3	2	1

What went well?

_____

_____

What needs work?

_____

_____

What surprised you?

_____

_____

The next time you do a Kidversation question, what do you want to do differently?

_____

_____

What does it mean to be popular at your school?

Question type: **School**

How can you guide the discussion?
Did you feel pressure to be popular or cool? As adults, we tend to want to think we are past such things, but think about whether you still have feelings carried over from your teenage years. We can often be haunted by our former selves and our pasts. Help your kids to understand how you've changed and grown past what you were.

Parent-to-parent...More insight
For better or worse, many parents tend to view their children's school experience through the lens of their own experiences. We remember what we went through and we want to see our kids do better, to be more popular, to be a better athlete. Here is a not so subtle hint. Stop. Now. Your kids are not you. They are fighting hard enough on their own, looking for their own self-definition, to also worry about your past issues. They are trying to find out who they are, popular or not, "hot" or not, etc. Helping them to feel safe and comfortable as themselves is a long, slow slog. Don't muddy it further with your own issues.

Supporting Questions
- How much do you think popularity matters once you leave school?

- Would you rather spend time with one really good friend, or a lot of friends all at once?

How did the conversation go?

Great		Fair		Poor
5	4	3	2	1

What went well?

_____

_____

What needs work?

_____

_____

What surprised you?

_____

_____

The next time you do a Kidversation question, what do you want to do differently?

_____

_____

Describe the cliques in your school.

Question type: **School**

How can you guide the discussion?
Depending on when and where you went to school, you might have had a vastly different experience than your kids. But if you think back, you can probably link your experiences to theirs. Where did you fit in your school's social spectrum? Is there anything about your experience that you would prefer not to share with your kids? Find a way to clean it up and then share. You can build trust and at the same time show them how time has changed you and your perspective.

Parent-to-parent...More insight
From jocks to geeks and everything in between, there have been cliques, labels, and groups in schools forever. Kids naturally come together, maybe because of common interests, maybe because of perceived common threats. Sometimes kids want to be in another group. Sometimes cliques can be a defense. A few things to remember. Kids often hate the word clique and will say they are not part of one but will accuse others of being 'cliquey.' And there is often tension and sometimes open hostility between cliques. By understanding the social environment at your child's school, you learn much more about their daily life.

Supporting Questions
- Why do you think that there are different cliques or groups in your school?

- Do you feel like you are friends with kids in different groups, or do you mostly stick to just one?

How did the conversation go?

Great		Fair		Poor
5	4	3	2	1

What went well?

_____

_____

What needs work?

_____

_____

What surprised you?

_____

_____

The next time you do a Kidversation question, what do you want to do differently?

_____

_____

What do you struggle with when doing homework? Your favorite parts?

Question type: **School**

How can you guide the discussion?
As with many other things, our own experiences tend to color how we view things with our kids. What were your homework experiences? Did you do well in school? Did things change between middle school, high school and college? If you can help your kids to understand why you believe grades are important, you can help them to understand why you push or plan to start pushing. At the same time, find out if you are driving them nuts, and then pull back and find a compromise.

Parent-to-parent...More insight
Homework is such a defining part of school life. Perhaps it is a constant source of argument or maybe a source of pride. For better or worse, grades matter. But if your child does poorly in school, homework can be at the root of many other problems such as poor self-esteem, behavioral problems, and on. And as a parent, you are most likely trying to balance wanting your child to do their best in school with the realities of family life. Homework can take a really long time, and it can be hard to get them to do it consistently. If you are struggling, the first step is open and honest communication. One suggestion: start with a planner (it can be as simple as a notebook or as complex as an online solution such as Google Calendar) that must be updated ever day. And get in touch with their teachers who can be an amazing resource.

Supporting Questions
- Is homework important? Why do you say so?

- What do you think is the connection between homework, schoolwork, and life outside school?

- What are three things you can do to make doing homework easier and more enjoyable?

How did the conversation go?

Great		Fair		Poor
5	4	3	2	1

What went well?

_____

_____

What needs work?

_____

_____

What surprised you?

_____

_____

The next time you do a Kidversation question, what do you want to do differently?

_____

_____